SOUL PURPOSE

SOUL PURPOSE

Rediscover your Creative Genius
and Become the Champion of your Life.

Jody Miller Stevenson

Source Communications & Publishing

Requests for such permission should be addressed to:

Source Communications & Publishing
6663 SW Beaverton-Hillsdale Hwy., #266
Portland, OR 97225
503-977-2235

Library of Congress Catalog Number: 95-070275

ISBN # 0-9646810-0-5

Printed in the United States of America
First Printing 1995

Book design by Alise Rubin
Cover design by Suzanne Stauss
Cover photograph by Susan Miles

Contents

Foreword

This book beautifully accomplishes many important things, but it cannot do the impossible. It cannot duplicate the full experience of a personal conversation with Jody Stevenson.

Perhaps I can help you capture something of that one-on-one experience. Here's what I suggest. As you read through the chapters, using the tools Jody describes so well, imagine that you are sitting opposite an attractive blond woman with extremely kind eyes. Jody gives you her complete attention with a focus that is almost unnerving. She is totally present to you, to the moment and to the topic at hand.

She smiles knowingly, quick to support or sympathize as you describe the woes of your life. And yet something in the warm but piercing gaze lets you know she may not be accepting your every complaint and excuse at face value. She will, however, quietly listen to everything you may need to say—even your most self-pitying complaints.

I suggest you keep talking for as long as possible, because if you leave even a tiny little silence for Jody to step into, the conversation is going to take a very different, distinctly unnerving turn. With a few simple questions she will firmly guide you into a new perspective. You will no longer be a victim. You will no longer be trapped, backed into a corner by the vagaries of life. You will be shocked to see doors appear in what had seemed to be solid walls blocking any forward movement.

Seems like good news, right? Well, yes . . . and no. You now have choices to make—which door should you try first? And it may be alarming to realize that the doors do not magically spring open with a wave of your hand. There's work to be done, and resistance to be overcome. But there at your elbow is Jody—probably more excited than you are at the possibilities unfolding in your life, and convinced that you are completely capable of the work at hand.

No book can duplicate that one-on-one experience. But this book comes very close.

Soul Purpose will change your life, if you are willing for that to happen. How that change expresses will be unique to you. We tend to think of change in terms of quitting our jobs, leaving our relationships, losing thirty pounds and heading for Sonoma in a Volkswagen camper—which is great if that's what you're called to do. But fear of that kind of drastic upheaval may keep us locked in uncomfortable but tolerable lives, trying to ignore the itch for something more.

If dramatic change is needed, this book will help you pack your bags. But dramatic change is not necessarily what *Soul Purpose* is about. Jody wants us to change our minds. She wants us to see possibilities instead of obstacles, opportunities instead of challenges.

Soul Purpose is about priorities and perspective. You may finish the book and find yourself changing absolutely nothing about your outer life—same job, same relationships, same hobbies and habits and hang-ups. But you will see everything differently; you will appreciate everything more, and your life will feel brand new.

There's something else you need to keep in mind as you embark upon this powerful book. And that is that Jody is not speaking here about lab-tested theories or abstract philosophy. Wherever you are right now in terms of low self-esteem, victim consciousness or total confusion about the choices and challenges of life, Jody has been there. She knows from personal experience how alluring it can be to settle for less than we really deserve, or to allow other people's opinions to destroy our dreams. She remembers well that taking the first step can seem paralyzingly difficult; but she also remembers how much easier the other steps are once that first one has happened.

And so, welcome to the loving, supportive and challenging consciousness of Jody Stevenson. It will change your life, because it will change your consciousness. By the time you finish *Soul Purpose,* you will have two new friends—Jody Stevenson, and yourself. Both are extraordinary people who will joyfully enrich your life.

Rev. Edward Townley, *Unity Minister*

To my sister Trish,
whose profound beauty
and understanding of life
is soul deep;
and
to my brother-in-law John,
whose wisdom and love of life
uplifts the consciousness of all humanity.

Acknowledgments

I have this vision of writing out a scroll that encircles the earth. On it would be a thank you for every person who has touched my life on a soul level, whether in a quick moment or one that lasts a lifetime. However, the task at hand is to acknowledge the extraordinary people who have shared their talents, skills and honesty so that *Soul Purpose* can have a breath of its own.

First of all, this book would not exist without my editor and book designer, Alise Rubin, *the Word Weaver*. I first met Alise when she was a student in one of my Right Livelihood classes. It did not take long for her extraordinary talent to reveal itself. I soon became one of her students. Alise's creative power is quiet, forthright and highly regarded. Thank you Alise for living your soul purpose so graciously.

Another person who deserves much gratitude is Suzanne Stauss, my book cover designer. Suzannne is a person who lives her life from the inside out. She knows who she is, what her talents are and she apologizes to no one.

Susan Miles, who created the cover photograph, is one of the most talented photographers I have ever met. *Soul Purpose* is indeed fortunate to be blessed by her magic touch.

I have been blessed with many friends, all of whom have contributed in one way or another to the creation of this book: Bonnie and Ken Ingersoll; Lela Bryan; Joanne McCall; Hermene Rinehard; Jeff Bornefeld; Jan Carothers; Cindy Roundtree; Gerry Warren; Blain Carlock; Reggie Robinson; Dorothy Dubia; Rev. Mary Shelton; Cheryl Long Riffle; Linda Swanson; Rev. Dr. Ernie Forkes, for being the best teacher I have ever had—and the toughest; Kristin Loomis; Dr. Jim Munson; Judy Pearson; Bill O'Hearn; Jae Allen; Rev. Mary Morrissey, and many others. A heartfelt thanks to Marcia Perkins-Reed, author of *When Nine to Five Isn't Enough* and *Thriving in Transition,* for so readily sharing her wisdom, encouragement and expertise.

We all deserve to have special friends who are ruthlessly honest and willing to dream big with us. I have such a friend. Mark Bosnian and I have been mastermind partners for seven years, and without his encouragement this book would not exist. A special thank you to Rev. Ed Townley, who refuses to listen to my limitations; and to my dearest friend, Jenna Watkins, who has given me the greatest of all gifts, the willingness to travel the soul journey with me. Thank you also to Brenda Petris for teaching me about boundaries, and to Rena Davis who quite literally saved my life.

There are three people, however, to whom I must give a roaring standing ovation: my two sons, Cam and Corey, who have taught me that love is the ultimate gift of life, and to my beloved husband, Al Miller, who is a master of nurture and support! I love you all very much!

Introduction

As I sat with my feet dangling over the rim of the Grand Canyon, the answer came to me. It was so obvious that I had to chuckle.

"Where have I been all these years?" I asked myself silently.

I was at another crossroads in my life. I knew I was going to be making some changes, but I was not sure what. As I looked out and saw the sun dance across the reddening rock of the far wall, I marveled at the power and intelligence it took to carve out these canyons.

I closed my eyes and heard the pounding of the Colorado River as it continued to carve out one of the greatest wonders of the world. (Nature certainly knows how to create extraordinary beauty!) I could see in my mind's eye the raging waters moving the earth and I felt the power of the Great Creator moving similarly in me. It was as though I could hear the spirits of the canyons saying, "That which created me is trying to create a life of beauty, depth and soul purpose through you."

Here I was, a top executive of a large organization; status, power and a good salary were mine. I was well known in the profession and by all appearances I had reached a major peak in my career. The only problem was, I was miserable. I had material abundance but was starving spiritually. I had been so outer-directed I had lost touch with my inner purpose, my god Self. My ego was over-fed and my soul malnourished.

In this moment I made the decision to follow my bliss. But what would bring me to my bliss? I knew I loved to teach and to speak. As I looked back through the pages of my life, I realized I could teach people about alcoholism, bulimia and incest recovery for I had experienced them all. I knew about workaholism, burn out and other compulsions. If being one makes one, then I was an expert on single parenting. Achieving prosperity, good relationships and better health were principles I had taught for years.

While I knew I could teach the world about these subjects, I felt little passion for them. As I reviewed my life, I realized that the Great Creator was nudging me to harness my creative energies and say yes to my true aspiration—to write!

"OK," I said, "Great Spirit, show me the way."

The privilege of a lifetime is to be yourself.

Joseph Campbell

In the next few minutes, my path to realizing my dream became glaringly clear. I'd been teaching a class called "Living your Right Livelihood" for years. I thought, I love working with people at their soul level, and so many people seem passionless, purposeless or confused about who they are.

"Teach people about their souls' purpose," I heard my inner voice say. "Teach through the written and spoken word, but by all means, *teach* and do it *now*."

When I returned home, I resigned from my job and began my inward journey. I took all the exercises and techniques I have taught for years and put myself through this course towards inner awareness with fierce determination. The exercises in this book come not from a theoretical base but from personal experience. I know they work because they worked for me.

Whatever your age, your income or your status in life, my wish for you as you read this book and work the exercises is that you feel more inspired and appreciative of who you are. It is my intention that you learn to recognize and promote your talents and your skills, and that you courageously pursue your dreams. Through my personal stories, I am inviting you into the mystical atmosphere of everyday life. It is in ordinary living that we experience the extraordinary expression of our soul selves.

Soul Purpose is to be used as a tool for self discovery. What you will find is that you exist for very special reasons and that who you are matters to the entire tapestry of humankind. Even if right now you don't believe you are creative, you *will* become aware of your tremendous creative powers. You will realize you are the sculptor, the director, the master, and the central character in your own life story, and you get to create your life exactly the way you want it. You will come to know that by divine inheritance you deserve to live abundantly, happily and with peace.

SOUL PURPOSE
Process of Creation

The symbol for the process of awakening one's soul purpose is the heart contained in the center of the lotus flower which sits inside a circle.

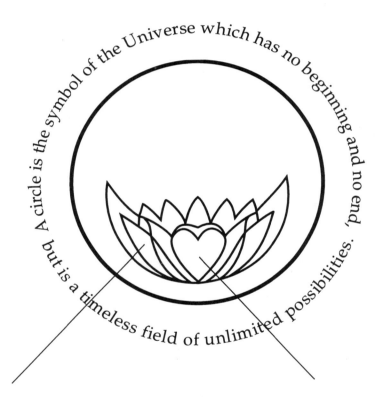

A circle is the symbol of the Universe which has no beginning and no end, but is a timeless field of unlimited possibilities.

Like the lotus flower, which emerges from the murky depths of the water to bloom, many lives of clarity and purpose arise from murky, dark beginnings to grow into exquisitely beautiful expressions of Life—the soul's process of awakening.

The heart represents the individual—the Self. At the heartbeat of every person resides one's soul purpose—unique, wonderful and powerful.

BEGINNINGS

Doorway Of Destiny

The awakening of my own soul's purpose began with a jolt twelve years ago. Little did I know when I started out that particular spring day that I would step from one energy field of reality to another. The person who woke up in my body that morning would not be the same one who would go to bed that night.

It was 10:30 AM and I was late for my appointment. I had a busy day ahead of me; my mind cluttered with the many tasks and errands I wanted to accomplish. As I hurried down the street in Seattle's Pioneer Square district, oblivious to my surroundings, I suddenly stopped, cemented in my tracks. Out of the corner of my eye, I noticed a flash of gold. Very slowly, life as I had known it began to change and I was about to experience the most freeing and healing moment of my life.

As I stood there, aware of the noisy cars and buses behind me, a man, dressed in a dark business suit and seemingly pursuing the important busyness of his life, passed in front of me. With irritation he yelled, "Hey, lady, get out of the middle of the damn sidewalk!" Coming the other way, a gray-haired old woman shuffled her grocery cart towards me. Her deeply wrinkled face and her ragged tan coat covering slumped shoulders told her story of pain and struggle. "Excuse me, honey," she said apologetically, "I gotta get by."

"Oh, oh excuse me," I responded absently as I moved aside.

It was then that the noisy hustle and bustle of the street became silent and time stopped. I stood there with my heart pounding and my body sweating, but I was unable to continue onward. That something momentous was about to happen was too obvious to miss even in my unaware state.

As I looked around I saw nothing unusual. There was only a dirty brick building, a man curled up in the doorway, and me. Why had I stopped? I looked closer at the man in the dirty rags who was curled up in the doorway. I didn't know him by the long, salt and pepper hair and scraggly beard. The torn, gold polyester shirt and dirty brown pants were unfamiliar to me. I had never seen the ripped shoes and green military overcoat he had rolled himself in to keep warm. It was the ring that had caught my attention. His hand was draped over the coat he was using as a blanket, and the sunlight had caused the ring to flash just as I walked by. How well I remembered that gold signet ring! I had seen it daily as a child on the hand of my father. Slowly I realized the man sleeping in the doorway *was* my father! *My Dad!*

As I looked at this man whose ears and neck were covered with lice, memories of a handsome, charming man came flooding back. I remembered how much he was sought after as a partner at elite country club dances. I recalled how important it was for him to be immaculate, clean-shaven and fashionably dressed.

Suddenly, it was as though a movie of my life passed in front of my eyes. I saw the long, dusty road leading to the circular driveway in front of the white rambler house with the heavy, dark blue, front door. I saw the parties—so many parties, and heard the people laughing, drinking and pretending. The big band sound was loud and clear. Then I recalled the violent fights at the dinner table night after night. The incest. The sarcasm. The divorce. And I remembered the good times. I saw Dad and me as we found the golden Easter egg at the club; the poem we wrote that won the honor of being published. Dad's remarriage. The private school. I saw the treatment center; I felt the hope of recovery. It all flashed before me.

I was grief-stricken and ashamed as the memories of yesterday came flooding back. The little girl inside me felt again the humiliation and embarrassment I had felt for so long. I angrily asked God, "Why my family? What's the purpose of all this? Why was my family hit so hard with alcoholism, drugs and abuse? There is no purpose, no purpose! Why?"

I stood there looking at my father with tears running down my face. The depth of pain seemed unbearable, and yet, in this moment I surrendered. I began to experience the most freeing and healing moment of my life. It was as though the plan for my life revealed itself to me and I began to understand the reasons it unfolded as it had.

When I reached this level of vulnerability, which I had never experienced before, the answer came. A deep wave of mystical understanding began to wash over me and the veil of separation was lifted. I understood that before me was a beautiful expression of life rediscovering his soul in his own way. Realizing I had no right to judge, analyze or condemn his life or anyone else's, I saw my father's life as perfect. I knew I had no need to worry about him or change him, even though I had spent years taking his inventory, criticizing him, trying to fix him and save him. Knowing who he was and finally seeing his perfection was an experience that changed my life forever. I realized that what looked like a long, downward journey from wealth and sophistication to skid row gutter living, was, on a spiritual level, a perfect journey of love in action.

In this moment of truth, I knew that there are infinite paths to knowing the Great Creator. My father was one of the most talented and creative men I have ever known, and his pathway of self-discovery was alcoholism, abuse and living on the streets. His path was perfect for him. I asked myself if I was willing to acknowledge my God-given creative talents and step boldly into my greatness, or whether I was going to continue to let drugs, alcohol, bad habits and fear of other's opinions rob me of my dreams?

To the question of your life, you are the answer. To the problem of your life, you are the solution.

Joan Cordeau

As I looked at this talented man curled up in the doorway of his destiny, I saw the perfection of life. I realized there is no right or wrong. Life is not black and white, filled with *shoulds* and *shouldn'ts.* Life just is. Through his personal journey, my father gave me the greatest gift there is—the gift of compassion.

The Cosmic Set-up

There are two things never promised or guaranteed in life: one is the promise of happiness, and the other is the promise of unhappiness. However, to a large degree, whether you are happy or unhappy is determined by how aware you are of your creative abilities, and the opinion you hold of these abilities. This book is about traveling our spiritual journey to greater awareness. The discovery of our *soul purpose* is more of a rediscovery or uncovering process because our soul purpose, the purpose for our existence, is already contained within us. Indeed, it is coded at the center of the DNA in every cell of our body.

M. Scott Peck, in his book *The Road Less Traveled,* states, ". . . it is possible for us to come to a deeper and deeper understanding of what our existence is all about. And gradually we can come to the place where we actually know what we are doing." Understanding what our existence is all about is to recognize there is a blueprint for perfection in each of us. This blueprint is our *soul purpose*; it contains the answers we seek in life and will be revealed to us step by step if we are willing to travel the journey of awakening.

The concept of having a spiritual journey is not to be confused with religious dogma. You will find nothing in this book that demands that you follow a specific path—that there is only one way and this is the way. A spiritual journey, as used in the context of this book, relates to the inner unfolding of your true nature.

Soul Purpose Principles

There are six basic principles to remember and embody as you travel along your spiritual journey to rediscovering your soul purpose.

The first soul purpose principle is that we *all* exist in a field of cosmic energy. At the heart of this creative energy is the Source from which all things, animate and inanimate, are created. It is an energy field of all possibilities. While this creative source may have many names—God, the Great Spirit, Yahweh, Allah, the Universe—and while there are many spiritual paths to the discovery of this energy—Christianity, Judaism, Islam, Buddhism, New Thought—there is, indeed, only *one* Source. This book will refer to the *One* as the *Great Creator*.

Divine Love is the source that creates and sustains this energy field in which we exist. All things that come into being are an expression of this divine love and there are an infinite number of ways to express love on the physical plane. Matter is the result of this energy taking on form. This divine energy cannot

Whatever your age, if you learn to listen, your inner voice will speak to you about your path, about your job on earth.

Bernie Siegel

be destroyed, damaged, degraded or worn out. This energy does not judge, condemn or discriminate one form of creation over another. It is intelligent in that it knows how to create form out of ideas and it is motivated only by love. It has created human beings to be partners with this divine energy in creating our lives, and has given us the ultimate tool of co-creation—our imagination.

The second soul purpose principle is that we are each unique expressions of the Great Creator. Our own set of talents, skills, loves, dreams and ideal audiences are combinations never seen before and never to be duplicated. In the truest sense, we are each completely original.

The third soul purpose principle is that by divine heritage, that by virtue of being unique and wondrous expressions of the Great Creator, we are destined to be joyous, love-filled, prosperous and healthy human beings. Pain, suffering, sickness, poverty, war and oppression are a result of our forgetting our connection to the Divine and our unwillingness to express our soul purpose.

The fourth soul purpose principle is to acknowledge that our soul purpose is the Great Creator's gift to us. Expressing our purpose and sharing our uniqueness is a joyful acknowledgment and return of this gift to the Great Creator. To live a life of service is the highest form of creative expression. It honors the soul and exults the spirit.

The fifth soul purpose principle is that as human beings, we are all connected at the soul level. As we look into each other's eyes, we see not only unique expressions of the Great Creator manifested in our individual bodies and personalities, but we also see the spiritual connectedness that makes us all one. Indeed, the Hindu word *namaste,* used as a salutation, means roughly, "The God in me acknowledges the God in you."

The sixth soul purpose principle, and perhaps the most important, is that all answers to any questions we may have—especially to those pertaining to our soul purpose—are found within us. When we are able hear the quiet voice within us, we have gained access to this wisdom and can use it to guide our lives.

Human beings are like islands in an ocean. As you look at the islands on the surface of the ocean, they look separate and different. Each is unique in its size, shape, topography and inhabitation. Yet, beneath the surface, each island is connected to the ocean floor, and therefore, to all other islands. So too are humans different and unique on the level of human expression, but each is connected at the soul level to the Great Creator and at that level we are all one. It is the desire of the Great Creator that we all live a life of meaning and purpose. Our job, when we are expressing our soul purpose, is to share our talents, skills and dreams with humanity to make this planet a safe and healthy place for *all* its inhabitants to live.

Sacred Triangle

The journey of awakening to the rediscovery of our soul purpose is simple, but not always easy. It is simple because the process consists of only three parts: willingness, awareness and action. It is not always easy because we are often missing one or more of the necessary elements in our lives.

Willingness

Willingness requires that we let go of inappropriate hard core beliefs, especially those regarding lack and limitation, lean into our resistance to change and step into a higher dimension of ourselves. In order to change, we must develop a life of discipline, mastering both our thoughts and actions. We must re-evaluate our priorities and willingly focus on the love in our lives and

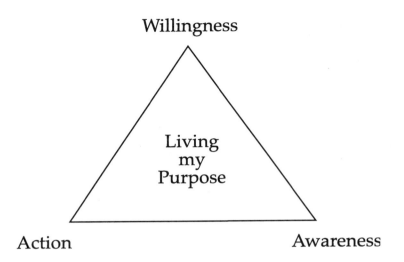

that which we choose to create. In our willingness to push the edges of our current reality, we begin to experience new aspects of our being of which we have usually not been aware. Willingness is a way to surrender our old self so that our true nature—our *soul self*—can be revealed.

Awareness

Awareness requires that we take a long hard look at ourselves. Our personal power comes from knowing our strengths, weaknesses, goals and dreams. The step to personal success are (1) to become aware of what we do best, (2) to determine what we want to develop in our lives, (3) to picture how we want our lives to be in the future, and (4) to determine how we want to get there. Awareness allows us to focus our attention on what we intend to create in our lives.

Awareness also requires that we be honest with ourselves. Are our thoughts and actions in alignment with our desires? Are we taking steps each day to move forward in realizing our dreams? Are we setting appropriate boundaries so that when we say yes we really mean it? Self-awareness gives us a clearly defined sense of our limitations as well as our strengths. Awareness is the key component to the realization of one's soul purpose.

Action

The Buddhist path reminds us that "a journey of one-thousand miles begins with a single step." This is true for the journey towards rediscovering our soul purpose. The spiritual practice put forth in this book is to take small, daily steps towards manifesting what we want in our lives.

Action also requires that we pay close attention to the details of our lives and that we create a clear picture of how we want our lives to become. As we do this, we will seek out those with whom we share mutual respect and appreciation, and we will develop a support system based on honesty, love and trust. Perhaps the greatest outcome of taking action is that we become directors of our own lives.

How to Use this Book as a Spiritual Compass

Let go of any expectations of what you have to do to awaken your soul purpose. There are no hard-and-fast rules, except that you do this with compassion and love for yourself. This book will present you with options to aid you in your process. Some of these you will enjoy; some you won't. Some exercises will expand your self-awareness; others might reveal nothing you don't already know. Some might push you, irritate you, perhaps even cause you some discomfort. Others may fill you with the happiness that comes from greater self-knowledge.

If you are not used to using your inner judgment, then start to use it now by assessing how you feel about a particular exercise before beginning it. If it feels right, then do the exercise; if it doesn't, this usually means it is the most important exercise you could do to assist in breaking through that which is holding you back. Also, let your inner wisdom guide the pace of your journey through this book. Let the process unfold at whatever pace is comfortable for you. There is no right or wrong way to travel the spiritual path of creative awareness. Keep in mind, however, the more focused you are, the more self-aware you will become.

As you work through this book and its exercises, do something daily which supports the rediscovery of your soul purpose. Read your Declaration of Soul-Purposed Expression (Chapter 2), or study your list of soul qualities (Chapter 3). Ask yourself repeatedly throughout the day, is the decision I am making in this moment supporting my well-being—the expression of my soul purpose, or is it feeding the dysfunctions of my limited self? Practice visualizing your future self expressing your soul's desires. Rediscovering and expressing your soul purpose is like learning any new life-style habit or skill: it takes focus, commitment and practice. It is a tool for greater self-awareness. Use it wisely and joyfully for at the end of your journey you will find the most precious gift of all—the authentic *you*.

Soul Purpose Principles

1.   We exist in a field of cosmic creative energy which is the source of all that exists.

2.   Divine love is the source of this cosmic energy field of possibility.

3.   We are each a unique expression of the Great Creator.

4.   It is our divine right to live lives filled with joy, prosperity, health and creative expression.

5.   Our soul purpose is the Great Creator's gift to us and expressing it is our way of honoring this gift.

6.   We are all inter-connected and by sharing our individual greatness, we uplift the consciousness of humanity as a whole.

7.   Our internal source of wisdom has all the answers we need to express our soul purpose.

SOUL PURPOSE DEFINED

What is Soul Purpose?

❖ *Soul* is the spiritual essence embodied in all human beings, a person's total self. This is sometimes called one's *true self* or *higher self*.

❖ *Purpose* is the reason, the intention for manifesting into human form.

❖ *Soul purpose* is an intention to express your spiritual essence—to express your total self in your life. When you are expressing your soul purpose, you have stepped into your *genius self*.

❖ *Genius self* is the state of living your soul purpose.

Soul purpose is the acknowledgment that you have unique talents and *only you* can express these talents. Other people may have similar talents, such as an ability to sing, write or organize, but only you can express these talents in your own special way. When we combine this truth with a willingness to serve humanity and give away these special talents, we experience the fullness of our soul purpose.

You, by virtue of your existence, have a right to live a healthy, joyful, prosperous and creative life. You have a right to be successful—in whatever way you define success. Rediscovering your soul purpose is a process of remembering what your intention is for your life. This process leads you from the state of believing that it is acceptable to live a life of deprivation (not having what you want) and limitation (not being what you want), to a state of believing in and experiencing your unique greatness and full potential.

A human soul may be thought of as an opening through which Infinite Energy is seeking a creative outlet.

Emmet Fox

To live successfully requires that we boldly step into our *genius self*—the purpose of our soul. Our genius is the part of us that is unique to us—those qualities that set us apart as individuals—our talents and our innate way of interacting with the world. At the same time, our genius self is also connected to the universal Source; it is wise and knowledgeable. When we are living in the state of our genius self, we easily and effortlessly express our unique talents and skills, and we know what we need to do to be successful.

A Mind Shift is Required

Rediscovering our soul purpose requires a mind shift. We need to define our personal reality in a different way than we have been taught to do throughout our lives. In western culture, most of us were programmed to define ourselves according to outer values—what others (our parents, teachers, religious leaders, friends, enemies) think of us; what others expect of us; what our society says we should or shouldn't be or do. We are taught that other people's opinions matter. We learned early on that who we are is determined by what we think others think we are! Our sense of self is limited and confusing, and further restricted by our addictions and compulsions.

As we awaken to our genius self, we discover that we are so much more than our physical bodies. The body is the vehicle through which our soul expresses itself in time and space, but it is not the totality of who we are. We are more than our bodies, but without a physical body, our creative energies would be unable to express and would remain dormant.

Rediscovering our soul purpose, then, requires us to change our view of ourselves—to cast away the definitions and restrictions of others and to redefine ourselves from the inside out. We need to find out who we truly are, what our unique talents are and how we want to express ourselves. Living our soul purpose requires us to consciously create life from the inside out. Within each of us is an infinite supply of creative energy seeking to be expressed and yearning to be experienced. Life's greatest mystery can be discovered only by listening to the ancient wisdom of our inner voice. The soul knows of journeys and new understandings that our human mind cannot yet fathom.

The Experience of Love

In this human experience called life, you and I exist for only one reason: to experience love. Love can be expressed as good health, joy, abundance, harmonious relationships, freedom of expression and other positive attributes. However, how we experience love is up to us, and the degree of love we have in our lives is determined by how open we are to accept it.

In all of our actions and thoughts, we are doing one of two things: extending love or putting out a call for love. When we are expressing anger, fear, sarcasm, hate or other negative emotions, we are actually asking to be loved, noticed and acknowledged. When we are expressing love, we are centered and happy, and extending from our genius selves.

Living from the Inside Out

Living our soul purpose requires us to consciously create life from the inside out. Within each of us is a rich, infinite pool of creative energy seeking to be expressed and yearning to be experienced. Life's greatest mystery can be discovered only by listening to the ancient wisdom-call of our inner soul's voice. The soul knows of journeys and understandings that our human mind cannot yet understand.

To create life from the inside out often requires that we change our beliefs about ourselves. Who we are today is the sum total of the beliefs we have been holding about ourselves. These beliefs have been ingrained in us since birth by our parents, family, teachers, religious leaders, friends and by our culture. They are both consciously and unconsciously applied to us over time like many layers of paint on a wall. By the time we are grown, we may have no idea what was the original color of the wall.

If your sixth grade art teacher once told you that you are not meant to be an artist, you may believe that you are not creative and may never have the courage to try to express yourself through art. The urge may be there; you may be drawn to artists as friends, or love to browse through art supply stores, but the belief that you are not creative may keep you forever on the artistic sidelines.

Beliefs have far-reaching consequences. They not only affect every area of our lives, they are also magnetic in energy. What we believe about ourselves—I am capable and accomplish what I set out to do, or conversely, I have limited capabilities and cannot be successful—attracts experiences that re-enforce those beliefs. Our beliefs, then, become self-fulfilling prophecies.

Personal Story

Characteristic of an incest survivor, I had developed harsh and destructive beliefs about myself. At a very young age, I had decided I was fat, frumpy and stupid. I felt subhuman—more of an object than a human being with deep feelings, talents and dreams. As early as the first grade, I began to have learning problems in school. By the time I was twelve, I was a full-blown bulemic and spent the next 15 years fighting the disease of binge-vomiting. I hated myself. I developed destructive habits as I desperately wanted to die, and I hated living in my body. I was totally unaware that within me was a beautiful, talented and powerful expression of the Divine.

Shortly after my 28th birthday, I joined Smokenders, a smoking cessation program. I was smoking 2½ to 3 packs a day and was there to learn how to quit. However, what I found was much more important. For the first time in my life, I heard someone say, "You have *choice* in life and you have the ability to change your beliefs."

This statement sparked a desire in me and slowly I started to reprogram my subconscious mind. "I love myself," I whispered in front of the mirror. "You are a powerful and talented person," I said silently throughout the day. "You deserve to be happy," I periodically reminded myself. But I didn't believe what I was saying. "Oh, yeh, you fat slob. You are so stupid," I would hear myself respond. "You are nice, and you have beautiful hair, but that's it, you stupid idiot." The battle to reprogram my belief system has been an ongoing daily process for me.

While I still have negative beliefs about myself, I now know I am a beautiful and unique expression of the Great Creator. I value my life and joyfully welcome each day. At the core of my being, I love who I am. I honor my talents and skills, and rejoice in watching the unfolding of my success. I believe at my soul level that I deserve to be healthy, prosperous and joy-filled. And I am.

Changing negative beliefs to positive ones is not always easy, but it is *always* possible. Develop a strong spiritual practice of self-love, accept professional and personal support when you need it, work to reprogram your subconscious mind daily and you can change your life.

Core Beliefs

Sometimes we are not aware of our basic beliefs about ourselves. Our core beliefs, developed during the early stages of our lives, are stored in our subconscious mind. Even though we are unaware of these beliefs, they have a strong influence on our behaviors and actions. If as a child you were given negative messages about yourself through abuse, neglect or an environment of conditional love, you may have developed core beliefs that you are not a good person. Therefore, you are not worthy of having happiness in your life, or of having financial abundance, good health or satisfying relationships. Because this is what you believe about yourself at a subconscious level, what you will attract into your life will be limitation in some or many areas of your life.

If you believe you can, or if you believe you can't, you are right.

Henry Ford

With beliefs like:

> I am not important
> What I do is never good enough
> I am a victim of circumstances
> I have no creative talent
> Life is a struggle

you will approach life hesitantly, succumbing to the pitfalls of others' opinions and criticism. While never lost, your genius self will remain hidden and your soul purpose will wait in quiet repose.

The ability to create more success in your life by awakening your inner genius and rediscovering your soul purpose is profoundly impeded by such beliefs. Your core beliefs have to be changed to positive, self-affirming beliefs, such as:

I am competent
I am powerful
I am a genius
I am unique
There is a special purpose for my existence
My creative expression is a gift to humanity.

The Inward Journey

Our soul purpose is hidden in the archives of our subconscious mind. Coded within the DNA of every cell in our body is the pattern, or intention, of our genius self. With positive beliefs, the impulse of your genius is ignited and your soul purpose is stirred. When this happens, you begin to experience a new level of success and fulfillment.

So, how will you know when you are becoming a soul-purposed person? What are the characteristics of a soul-purposed person? How can you recognize when another is living according to his or her soul purpose? Of course, there is no one way that soul-purposed people behave as we are all unique expressions of the Great Creator, but there are some characteristics that I feel are typical of many soul-purposed individuals. (See page 20. At this point, I will simply list these characteristics as they will be explained in context throughout the book.)

But What if I Don't Know What My Soul Purpose Is?

Inevitably, someone in my workshops on soul purpose will come to me with a look of frustration and pain, and say, "All this sounds

Characteristics of a Soul-Purposed Person

People who live their lives based on soul purpose principles exhibit the following characteristics:

❖   Live life based on freedom and make decisions in support of this spiritual quality.

❖   Believe there is an extraordinary power within and create an outrageous vision based on this power.

❖   Expand an awareness of their divine gifts and continue to develop the skills, talents and dreams needed to express these divine gifts.

❖   Create a strong foundational support system.

❖   Develop a deep, inner life of prayer based on the recognition that we live in a field of infinite possibilities, and consciously choose their experiences.

❖   Know that their authentic boss is the Great Creator and are willing to take responsibility for putting more meaning into work.

❖   Refuse to work for money and recognize work is for the purpose of creative expression, but are willing to be richly rewarded for this expression.

❖   Are willing to forgive others, and most importantly, themselves, for past mistakes.

❖   Live a simple and disciplined life of service to humankind.

great, Jody, but what if I don't know what I want to do with my creative energies?" My response? I respectfully say to my student, "I totally understand; I have been there. I know how frustrating it is to have all this creative talent and energy and not know what to do with it. However," I say with a bit of hesitation, "Your not knowing what you want is due to the fact that you are full of negative B.S!"

At this point, the person usually looks at me with disbelief and alarm, so I explain, "B.S. is for BELIEF SYSTEM. You have within you the belief that you are unworthy of knowing what your soul purpose is. And because of your negative belief system, one of two things is happening: either you are not paying attention to the clues constantly being sent to you, or you are immobilized by fear and take no action."

Paying Attention to Details

Our daily lives are filled with little details that can be sign-posts on our voyage to self-discovery if we only learn to see them. The Great Creator is continually sending us messages through our dreams, our intuition and our flashes of awareness. When you are driving, do you notice what you are thinking about? How about when you fold laundry, walk the dog, stack wood or any other task that takes less than your full attention. Most of the time, we do these routine tasks on auto-pilot and our minds are off thinking about other things. Become aware of what you think about when you are occupied with routine things. That is the first step to recognizing the clues being sent to you.

The second step is to begin to notice who and what you are attracting into your life: what magazines and books do you read? What newspaper articles or TV news flashes grab your attention? What are your interests telling you? A friend of mine used to work in the corporate world. She has an MBA, was doing well and rising in the corporate structure. But she could rarely force herself to read business materials and didn't like to hang around

people who talked business. Whenever she reached for a magazine or book, it was always something to do with nature,
psychology, metaphysics or personal growth. As her frustration
continued to grow, it became inescapably clear that her interest
really wasn't in business and she needed to make a drastic change
in her career. She spent some time in the search and eventually
found her perfect career. She is now my editor!

What about the people you attract? These can be friends, ca-
sual acquaintances or perfect strangers. Have you ever had the
experience of someone you don't know blurting out the answer
to a problem you've been silently working on? Or maybe you
are at a friend's house and a neighbor walks in and starts talking
to you and you suddenly get the feeling—I'd better pay attention; I don't know why, but there's something here for me. Sometimes, the kinds of people we attract can send us a message. Do
you hang around actors a lot but aren't one yourself? Better take
a look at your secret desires. There may be an actor inside trying
desperately to get out. Are you fascinated by car-racing and auto
mechanics, and love to tinker with old cars? Perhaps there is a
message hiding here for you.

A third way to become aware of the messages being sent to
you is to put yourself into your ideal future and see what kind of
pictures, thoughts and feelings you get. Don't self-censor when
you do this. Watch the movies in your mind without analysis or
discussion, as though you were in a theater watching the show.
Let yourself be whatever comes to you. It is a way of trying out
the future without risk. Do this regularly and see what messages
keep repeating themselves. (I go into how to do this in more detail in an exercise called *VAK to the Future* in Chapter 4.)

By paying attention to the details of your life, you will receive meaningful messages that can become sign-posts in your
search to know your soul purpose. Life wants to express success,
joy, prosperity and love through you, and it will bring to you all
that you want and need to fulfill your dreams.

Positive Power

The second reason you may not know what you want to do with your life is because your fear factor is so high you can't get a clear sense of yourself, or it keeps you from taking action. So far, in the hundreds of workshops I have conducted, there is always someone who bashfully nods his or her head in agreement. Fear of Success? Fear of Failure? Fear of public opinion? Hog Wash! We have all had successes in our lives, and we have all had moments when we felt we failed. Public opinion controls us only if we still have a lot of co-dependency issues. What we are most fearful of is our own power! Let me repeat that: *We are really only afraid of our own personal power!*

What is personal power? When I ask my students how they behave when they are powerful, I often get answers like, "Oh, I'm rude, manipulative, controlling. I don't like to be powerful and I don't like to be around powerful people." This is an expression of negative power. Power that controls or coerces others, and is self-centered, is negative power. Most students say they don't know how to use their power positively.

Power, by definition, means to ". . . have the ability to act or produce an effect." Wouldn't you like to have the ability to act or produce the effects you want in your own life? In other words, be powerful rather than powerless? Positive power is being in charge of your own life. Being powerless is letting others control your life. Positive power is expressing who you really are in spite of what others think about you. Negative power is hiding who you truly are so that others will approve of you. Positive power is taking care of your own needs in ways that do not negatively impact others. Negative power is misusing or manipulating others to get what you want. A powerful person is vibrant, excited about life, speaks with authority and is of service to others. Powerless people are bored with life, speak with a whine and think only about themselves. Their troubles are big and important, and their sense of self is small.

To create our lives with a lack of conscious awareness is to put us in the victim role, to render us powerless. When we allow others to determine how we live our lives, we live other people's dreams instead of our own. If you are more concerned about what Mom, Dad, your spouse, your boss or the neighbors think of you than what you think of yourself, you are stuck in the victim, or co-dependent, mentality. Our choice, then, is simple: either remain a victim or choose to be powerful.

So, to rediscover your soul purpose, watch where your belief systems lead you, pay close attention to the details of your life, and be willing to move past your fear of being powerful.

Characteristics of a Soul Purpose

There are three basic aspects of soul purpose that will help you recognize when you have found yours. They are:

❖　**Your soul purpose is bigger than you.**

The thought of trying to accomplish your soul purpose must seem impossible for you to accomplish on your own. It can make your heart pound and your hands sweat just thinking about it, but if, in spite of this, you still passionately desire to accomplish your dream, then it is your soul purpose.

❖　**Your soul purpose excites you.**

While the idea of accomplishing your soul purpose may frighten you, the thought of attaining or becoming your dream is exactly what you want.

❖　**Your soul purpose serves humanity in some way.**

It is not a self-centered or selfish goal. It need not be as dramatic as joining Mother Theresa in India, or giving away all your worldly possessions to the poor, but your soul purpose is in some way of benefit to the planet or some portion of the rest of humanity.

If you absolutely have no clue as to what to do with your creative energy, go out and volunteer where there is a need. Extend a hand; offer a kind word to someone who is down on their luck; serve in a homeless shelter or a hospice; tutor in the schools. The list of needs is endless. Become bigger than your "I don't knows." Get outside of yourself and you will begin to recognize what you are drawn to—what excites you. If you continue to explore, your soul purpose will be revealed to you.

My Personal Experience

The two years before I entered ministerial school were very challenging and frightening years for me. My journey began with a recurring dream from which I would abruptly wake in a cold sweat. I kept dreaming I was in an airplane that was shooting straight up. Then in the next scene, I was standing in front of hundreds of people speaking. Night after night I dreamed this same dream.

During this same period, I was haunted by the idea that I wanted to be a minister even though I couldn't even say the word *God* without choking. It made no sense to me. I would be at the grocery store taking mayonnaise off the shelf and think, "Someday I'm going to be a minister." Or I'd be in the middle of a conversation with my husband, talking about what we were going to do on Saturday, and I'd say, "Honey, someday I am going to be a minister." The thought haunted me.

The clincher came one day at a party where I knew very few people. I starting talking to an older man. He was delightful, charming, witty, full of life, knowledgeable about many things, and obviously happy. As the conversation progressed, that inevitable question was asked, "And what do you do for a living?"

"I teach people about addictions and behavioral modification," I replied. "And what do you do?"

"Oh, I am a minister," he joyfully replied.

I remember the feeling I had as though it happened two minutes ago. Hot energy surged through me. My face became bright red and I panicked. "I'm being possessed. It's everywhere," I thought. "Damn-it, God," I said on the way home, "I will do anything but be a minister. I don't know how to be one!"

Shortly after that night, I told my sponsor at Overeaters Anonymous that I felt this strong urge to become a minister, but swore that if she told anyone, I would make her life unbearable. She laughed and said, "Of course, you want to be a minister, Jody; it's the perfect profession for you. In fact, I know where you will go to school. Let me tell you about it."

At this point I surrendered. The direction of my life could not have been clearer to me. The Universe moved in quickly after that and my life changed dramatically. I went to ministerial school and eventually settled happily into my own church.

The point of my story is this—by paying close attention to the details of your life, and by being willing to step into your personal power, you will receive clarity on what your soul purpose is, and you will find the strength and guidance to move forward and create exactly what you want in your life.

Declaration of Soul-Purposed Expression

Rediscovering your soul purpose is an inward journey of awakening. It is the greatest journey you will ever travel, filled with the promise of self awareness; the promise of a deep, peaceful, inner silence; and the promise of creative energy expressed. Rediscovering your soul purpose awakens you to your greatness, your uniqueness, your passions. The journey is yours for the asking; the promise is yours for the receiving.

As the first step to moving into the expression of your soul purpose, write out for yourself the Declaration of Soul-Purposed Expression and place it where you can review it daily. (See example on page 28.) Read this declaration each day with passion, and begin to incorporate these statements into your life. Use them to help you shift your mind and change your belief system to thoughts that support your growth into the true expression of your soul purpose.

Declaration of Soul-Purposed Expression

I, ———————— , declare that I am a unique, divine expression of Life. I remember that I have a soul purpose and I daily practice living my life guided by my true self. I am free to laugh, cry, change my beliefs, grow and feel my life fully. Because I choose to create my life from my soul's purpose, I declare the following:

❖   I free myself from blame. I recognize that I co-create my life with the Great Creator. I release the dependence I have on any person, place, thing, old belief or pattern, and I boldly step into the power of my creative abilities.

❖   I free myself from the judgments I have about others, and especially about myself. I think only loving, positive thoughts. I consciously think the thoughts I want to have happen to me, knowing that what I focus on expands in my life.

❖   I free myself from the attachments that are holding me back from living a life of freedom. I attach myself firmly to my soul purpose and courageously step into my destiny.

❖   I free myself from being a victim. I recognize that all past situations occurred for my greater good, and I accept responsibility for the learning.

❖   I free myself from worrying about my future and feeling guilty about my past. I live my life passionately and fully in the present moment, and look for the joy of life in every breath.

❖   I freely give thanks, moment by moment, as I boldly step into my divine life of living my soul purpose.

_____   _____
Signature   Date

REDEFINING YOUR LIFE

Choices

It was a typical winter day in Portland—the gusty, cold wind was pounding the rain against the window and I was engrossed with a project on my computer.

"Mom!" I heard this noise rattling against my concentration. "Mom, can you drive me back to school? I want to play basketball with my friends."

"Nope, I sure can't," I said to my computer screen.
"Mom, ple-e-ease!"
"No, I'm busy," I said to my older son, Cam.

"Mo-o-o-o-m, come on, please! You never do anything for me . . . basketball is good exercise. Please, Mom. Besides, I can feel it in my bones. I can feel you are going to joyfully choose to take me back to school. I can really feel your choice to support me, love me and honor me. Please, Mom?" He was giving me a dose of my own philosophy.

I slowly turned away from my computer to face him. He was leaning against the fireplace wall with arms crossed and a scowl on his face. "Cam, it may not be obvious to you, but I am working on something important, and besides, it's pouring outside right now. If you want exercise, go clean out the garage. It's one of your chores, anyway."

I could see Cam's anger rising. He kicked the fireplace and threw his hands up in utter frustration.

"You know, Cam, I see that you are angry and hear your frustration. I acknowledge that, but the feelings you are having are your responsibility. You see . . . ," I was winding up for a long sermon, "a long time ago when you were a soul, you were looking for a set of parents you could use as a vehicle to create a body, and you chose your Dad and me because we would provide you with the lessons you'd need to learn in this life. So, you knew when you chose me that I would not say yes to your every desire, that there would be times when I'd frustrate, bug and bother you. And yet, my dear son, you knew on a deep soul level that I was the right mother for you. You did choose me to be your mother." I tried to keep the ministerial look of authority out of my face.

Cam rolled his eyes, smiled, and without hesitation, said, "But, Mom, you were the last one on the list!"

We both broke up laughing and the tension dissipated. This event has since become an endearing joke between us. And a lesson in truth was embodied in this exchange.

It is from the soul level of our being that we create our life in this physical world. There is no point on the path of eternity where we are victims, or where we do not have choices. If you make choices based on outer world values and desires, you are creating your life from the level of your personality and you are maintaining the illusion of separation from Spirit. This is not necessarily a bad thing to do, but it will not get you where you want to go. Learn to make choices based on the impulses of your soul purpose in order to express with authenticity.

As human beings, we each make thousands of choices daily, both consciously and unconsciously. All choices are important and have a vibrational effect on our life. In fact, as you scan the life you have lived and describe what your current life looks like, you will vividly see the pattern of choices you have made up 'til now. If you don't like how your life has turned out, begin to choose differently. For every decision you make today, ask yourself, "Is this decision going to support my soul purpose or is it going to support my dysfunctions?" From this higher level of awareness, you will then begin to make healthy choices based on your well-being. When you do this, you change your life.

It is the big choices we make that set our direction. It is the smallest choices we make that get us to the destination.

Shad Helmstetter

As we grow in awareness of our inner-most needs and desires, our choices change. We become aware of the negative influences in our lives and we can stop giving them focus and attention. We remember that each choice we make has an impact on the quality of our life, and so we begin to rid ourselves of the negative and invite in only those things that empower, enhance and encourage our well-being.

Rescuing You from Yourself

I have gone out to look for myself.
If I should get back
before I return,
please hold me until I get there.

Anonymous

The swell of authentic self-expression is rising in America. By the beginning of the next millennium, most of us will practice a higher degree of personal power than we are doing today, and we will be aware of our genius selves.

To recognize our genius is to realize that within each of us is an enormous pool of creative power. We have the ability, wisdom and knowledge to create any level of success we choose. But for many of us, the creative genius is like a young, untamed child. It has been unleashed but is undisciplined; it desperately needs loving parental guidance.

Hundreds of people from around the country have approached me, often with a sense of frustration and despair, and said with a sigh, "OK . . . OK, I keep hearing I am this great powerful person who has the ability to create more success in my life . . . but where do I begin!"

Mind Power

We build our fortune thought by thought,
For so the universe was wrought,
Thought is another name for fate:
Choose then the destiny and wait,
For love brings love and hate brings hate.

Van Dyke

The power of your creative genius is your mind. Your thoughts have a constant vibrational effect on your life. What you think about today creates your tomorrow. It is that simple. Take conscious control of your thinking and you have the beginnings of a new life.

Many people don't want to hear this. I had the same reaction. When I first began to understand how powerful my mind is, I realized how many negative thoughts I had about others, and especially about myself. Then in a state of denial, I made a deal with my mind. I decided that practicing positive thinking 100% of the time was too big a challenge. So I told myself I could think 100 negative thoughts each day and they would NOT have a negative effect on my life. It didn't work. The creative energy of life responds to our thinking 100% of the time.

Thinking positive thoughts all day long, with every breath we take, is like a prayer. All the great masters have reminded us to pray unceasingly—in other words, think kind, loving, possibility thoughts instead of dark, negative ones. Having the willingness to step out from negative thoughts into positive, creative thinking shifts you from being a victim to a genius. The choice is yours.

Create Your Future from Your Present Thoughts

Most people have the habit of creating their present reality from their past—recreating time and time again, day after day, a life of mediocrity, lack and limitation. Science tells us we think approximately 60,000 thoughts in a given 24 hour period. Dr. Deepak Chopra, author of *Ageless Body, Timeless Mind*; *Perfect Health* and others, says, ". . . this figure is not astonishing. What is so astonishing is that 90% of those thoughts are the same ones we had yesterday." As we allow our inner genius to emerge and our soul purpose to reveal itself, we realize there is great power in creating our present reality, not from the past, but from the future.

Who we will be in five years, without the effort of genius creation, is determined by two current factors: who we associate with and the ideas we hold on to. When you evaluate your current life and decide you want it to continue just the way it is, you now know that if you continue thinking 90% of the same thoughts you thought yesterday and today, reading and listening to the same sources, and associating with the same people, you will have almost the same existence in the future as you do now.

Some of you will consciously decide to make changes in your lives, while others will decide to keep things the way they are. Some of those who are reluctant to change will experience what I call *divine discontent*—a feeling of restlessness, edginess and irritability without any apparent cause. As you look around your life, you won't be able to find anything wrong, but you will remain dissatisfied. This divine discontent is your genius self nudging you to go to the next level of your soul purpose. Whether you choose to change or remain the same, it is wise to keep a close watch on your thinking. By doing this, you rescue yourself from unintended results and the accompanying drama, trauma and chaos. As you practice noticing your thoughts, you will learn to trust your own feelings, focus your thinking and create a life of genius.

Living a Life of Freedom

Whenever we look outside ourselves to define who we are, we lock ourselves into the bondage of what others think of us. We immediately limit ourselves and begin to lose touch with the wisdom of our soul. The ultimate life of freedom is lived when we recognize that within us is our soul nature. It is the essence of you—your talents, your dreams, your uniqueness. Your soul self has the perspective of your eternal life and can guide you in your everyday life.

Living a life of freedom comes from the recognition that your thoughts determine your life. Everything you have experienced and achieved in your life was first a thought. But thoughts, by themselves, have no power. But give a thought focus, imagination and action, and you have a physical happening. Soul freedom is knowing and properly using the power of your mind.

You become a magnetic field of attraction through your thoughts. Whatever you most often picture in your mind, speak about in your internal and external conversations, and feel in your heart today, you are creating for tomorrow. *A Course in*

To change, we have to redefine our self and our priorities, to give ourselves permission to observe where we are without being defensive or judgmental about our point of view. We facilitate the next step on our path when we note our present position uncritically.

Wayne Dyer

Miracles tells us, "You have been endowed with a great and marvelous gift. Your thoughts are the key to your freedom. You who would reclaim your divine inheritance must do so through your thoughts."

To create a life of freedom requires an image and a focus. An image is a clear and detailed picture of your life of freedom. What do you look like? What do the detailed aspects of your life look like? What are the sounds you hear? What exactly do you feel? Imaging is an ancient art and has been used by healers throughout time to bring forth what was needed.

Focus requires discipline. This is not a nasty word. It is derived from the medieval word "disciple" which means "to teach or to train." Discipline is needed to maintain your vision and to take the steps necessary to make what you picture a reality.

The ultimate human freedom is the ability to choose how we will respond.

Victor Frankl

Freedom is experienced when we listen to the call of our inner voice leading us to express our soul purpose. We feel free when we can face our fears and go out into the world to use our talents and skills. How well we respond to our inner guidance determines how brightly we express our soul purpose.

Soul Qualities

✻ ***Soul qualities*** are aspects of life that you value, and that you want or already have in your life.

Imagine this:

> *You walk into a gigantic supermarket with unlimited products to buy - UNLIMITED. The products, uniquely created, represent qualities of life—qualities that can make up YOUR ideal life, like freedom, balance, creativity, security, health. With great excitement, you scan the building.*

You notice there is a sale table over on the other side of the room. A big sign reads, "90% MARK-DOWN." On this table are discontinued qualities like lack, fear, anger and limitation. You also notice that thousands of people are buying these qualities because they are cheap, and because owning these qualities makes them feel like they belong to a larger community—a community made up of struggling people, but a community, nevertheless.

Just as you gather your grocery cart, and decide you want all the positive qualities you can get, a grocery clerk walks up to you. With surprise, you note how much he or she looks like you, only this person is happier, healthier and is living more abundantly. The clerk lovingly reminds you he or she is your genius self. You listen. He or she then tells you that you are allowed to choose only eight qualities off the shelf—eight life qualities that you hold most precious or that you would like to have in your life. You consider carefully before choosing those eight qualities.

This process of choosing the eight qualities most essential to you allows you to determine what is most valuable in your life. We live in an energy field of unlimited possibilities. There are unlimited numbers and combinations of qualities available to you. The choices that are right for you will not be the same as those that are right for someone else, because what you want to manifest in your life will be different from what others want to manifest. Your life looks different because the qualities you hold to be valuable are magnetic for your life, and the qualities another holds to be valuable are magnetic for that person's life, and they are not the same. Even if we have the same list of qualities, the order or the value we place on each would be different. In my classes I have never seen one list of life qualities duplicate another.

Choosing Your Eight Soul Qualities

What you think about is drawn to your life. What you focus on in life expands. Whether you are consciously or unconsciously focusing, you are creating your life from the focus of these qualities. Life, in its simplest physical denominator, is energy. When you focus your attention on your soul qualities, you concentrate your life energy on them and help to bring them into your life.

An unexamined life is a life not worth living.

Socrates

Life in its simplest spiritual denominator is love. Love is the umbrella for many other qualities. The following is a list of possible qualities you might hold to be most valuable in your life.

Freedom
Health
Prosperity
Balance
Security
Sense of Belonging
Joy
Adventure
Honesty
Authenticity
Creativity
Fun
Purpose
Beauty
Naturalness
Faith

Trust
Peace
Alone-time
Play
Integrity
Wisdom
Expression
Confidence
Cooperation
Independence
Commitment
Discipline
Vision
Openness
Material Wealth

There are many others you can choose from.

As you look at the above list and add to it, begin to formulate your eight soul qualities list. Choose eight qualities that would make your life happier, more successful, more prosperous or more joy-filled. Now, write them down. (See the example on the next page.)

Soul Qualities I Want/Have in My Life
Example

1. (_1_) Excellent Health
2. (_6_) Independence
3. (_4_) Loving relationships
4. (_5_) Joy
5. (_2_) Balance
6. (_3_) Creativity
7. (_7_) Adventure
8. (_8_) Financial Wealth

This exercise is a powerful tool for self awareness. When you have decided what your eight qualities are, focus on the top three and begin to ask yourself if the decisions you are making in your life support the qualities you hold to be most valuable. Notice when and where you are creating your life outside of the boundaries of your integrity—in other words, when you are saying yes when you should be saying no. When we do this, we are denying ourselves the right use of our creative energies, our time and our soul purpose.

The hardest thing I have ever had to do is to follow the guidance I have prayed for.

Albert Switzer

As you study your list, you will begin to define yourself. As you begin to define yourself, you will begin to get in touch with your soul purpose—the genius self that says, " this is who I am and what I stand for." Soul qualities are the heartbeat of your soul's expression. By getting in touch with what you hold to be true, you allow yourself to see how and why you are creating the life you have.

A Personal View

In my experience, no matter how many times I complete this

process, *freedom* always lands in the first spot. This is important information. In order for me to express my creative energies, I know I have to feel free. I have to be able to come and go as I please and set my own schedules and time lines. This alone tells me I am more suited to be self-employed than working for someone else.

Creativity is another soul quality that I hold in the highest regard. This tells me I am more of an idea person than a detail person. While I was the Senior Associate Minister of a large church responsible for administering the ministry program, I realized I was in the wrong job. The part of me that is creative and innovative was screaming for my attention as I was required to focus on managing a myriad of details for many events. This job was not a good fit for me as I am more the visionary than the detail chaser.

Balance is another quality that is important to me, although it has not always been so. Since I have made balance one of my top three soul qualities, I hold my private time and my family time as important as service time with others. Since I have incorporated this value in my life, I feel much more centered, peaceful and healthy.

Soul Qualities Affirmation

When you have completed your Soul Qualities List, set it aside and check it every day or so. When you feel comfortable that your list truly reflects those qualities you want or have in your life, create a Soul Qualities Affirmation and put it in a prominent place. (See example on page 40.) Meditate on your soul qualities and use them to check whether your life choices support your chosen qualities.

Soul Qualities Affirmation

I, _____ , am _____ and
  Name   *Quality 1*
_____ , and _____ . I create life
      Quality 2   *Quality 3*
with the inner focus of _____ and _____ .
                              Quality 4   *Quality 5*
I know that only good can come into my life; therefore, I live in an

energy field of _____ and _____ . Because
                    Quality 6   *Quality 7*
I am a unique expression of the loving Universe, I joyfully experi-

ence _____ in my life.
          Quality 8

I willingly let go and trust Life, knowing that the impulse of Life
provides for me all that I need, and want and am able to accept. I
give thanks for the realization that within me is the genius of my
soul purpose. I recognize that I co-create my outer life from the power
of my soul qualities, and for this I give thanks for the privilege of
being me. And so it is . . . . Thank you, Life!

_____   _____

Signature   Date

Sacred Circles

Sacred circles are a tool for self awareness. They begin to create a map of the subconscious mind, gradually revealing aspects of ourselves of which we often are not aware. Just as great treasures of wealth have been discovered in the caverns of the earth, so too will we find great pearls of truth in the caverns of our minds— the greatest being our soul purpose.

While sacred circles appear to be a simple technique, it has the potential to initiate profound changes in a person's life. Many times in my classes I've watched students complete these circles and say, "I didn't know this about myself . . . and yet this feels so right." The insights revealed in the sacred circles encourage people to make needed changes in their lives.

In order for our genius self to step boldly into the light of authentic purpose, it has to feel safe. For many reasons we have learned it is safer to hide our true selves deep within our hearts rather than reveal ourselves. As children, we made decisions about who we are based on outside programming and perceptions. Unaware or wounded parents, teachers, friends and family have an enormous impact on whether we dare to reveal our soul purpose. Insensitive comments from hurried parents, ruthless opinions from peers, biased comments from insensitive teachers determine how safe it feels for us to boldly step forward and say, "This is who I am." Completed sacred circles offer a safe place to reveal yourself and often ignite courage, self respect and passion to move forward in your quest for self-discovery.

Guidelines for Creating Sacred Circles

There are six guidelines for using the sacred circles:

1. Create a safe atmosphere. Light a candle; say a blessing; state an affirmation. As with any journey, sending forth prayerful energy is helpful to insure a safe return.

2.   Thank your Critical Voice (that voice inside you that regularly tells you what it thinks of you and your behavior) for its constant sharing, and ask it to leave for a while. While the critical voice, if trained, can be quite useful for discernment purposes, it has no place in this process. *You cannot complete the sacred circles incorrectly!!* So send your Critical Voice on a vacation, and reassure it that it will be welcome back later.

3.   As with the Critical voice, the Analyzer is also not wanted. Its purpose is to probe, prod and logically analyze all the details of your life. While useful at times, it is counterproductive during the sacred circles process. So tell the Analyzer to accompany the Critical Voice on that vacation, and reassure it that it will be welcome back.

4.   Call forth your Observer Self—the part of you that only notices what goes on in your life, without judgment, analysis or opinions. The Observer is needed during the sacred circle process.

5.   Invite your Creative Child to join the sacred circle process. The Creative Child—your untamed, passionate, wild and gutsy self—knows no limitations or fear. He or she will boldly step into the unknown and will determine the depth of your self-discovery.

6.   Most important, extend an invitation to your True Self to participate, for your True Self has the knowledge of your soul purpose.

The First Sacred Circle

The first sacred circle is entitled "Things I Love to Do." Start at the top of the circle and write down all the activities you love to do—personally and professionally. If your activity has more than one component to it—for example, "I love hiking" is a general category, but the Appalachian Trail is your very favorite hiking spot, then add "the Appalachian Trail" as a secondary line coming off from your activity line. You can add as many secondary lines as you want. As you go around the circle clockwise, keep writing down what comes to you—without censoring or judging the responses. Feel free to add more lines or create another circle if you need to. Some ideas to get you started are:

> hiking
> horseback riding
> organizing
> managing people
> speaking in public
> sitting by the fireside with my loved ones
> drinking Starbucks coffee
> petting my cat

See the Things I Love to Do Sacred Circle example on page 44.

The Second Sacred Circle

The second sacred circle is entitled "Developed Skills." *Skill*, by definition, means " the ability to use one's knowledge effectively and readily in execution or performance . . . to make a difference." Developed skills are those abilities you have either learned through life experience or studied in school. Some ideas for recognizing your skills are:

> nursing
> listening
> organizing
> writing
> riding horses
> managing people
> observing people and nature

You may notice that the first and second circles contain some of

the same items. This is okay.

See the Developed Skills Sacred Circle example on page 46.

The Third Sacred Circle

The third Sacred Circle is entitled "Innate Talents." *Talent*, by definition, means "the natural endowments of a person." Innate talents are those things that you love to do and that you have a natural ability or inclination to do. Your innate talents may or may not have been refined through training. The use of your talents usually requires a blend of both your intellect and intuition. Some ideas for recognizing your talents are:

> skiing
> listening
> speaking
> auto-mechanic abilities
> athletics
> gardening
> painting
> singing
> working with children

See the Innate Talents Sacred Circle example on page 47.

The Fourth Sacred Circle

The fourth sacred circle is entitled "Visionary Dreams." Each of us has secret things that we would love to have, things that we would love to do and ways that we would love to be. These are our "If only I could . . ." or "Gee, I sure would love to . . ." dreams. Visionary Dreams lead us to begin exploring our impossible dreams—to give them form, reality, and a breath of life. While doing this process, be outrageous, write down the unthinkable. Some ideas to help you discover your visionary dreams are:

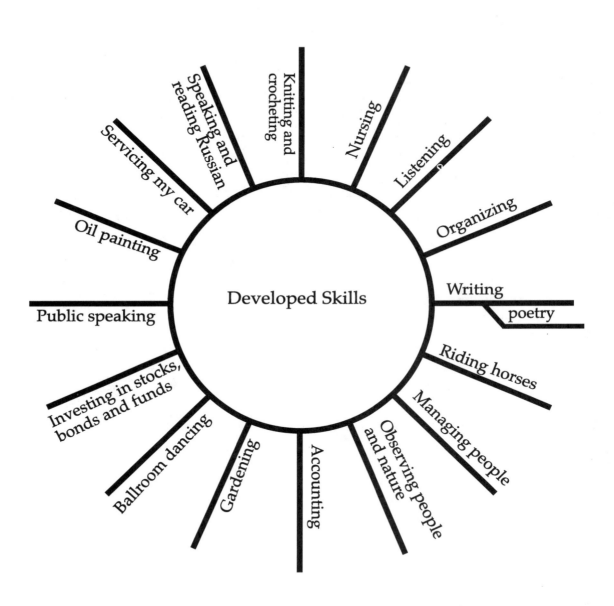

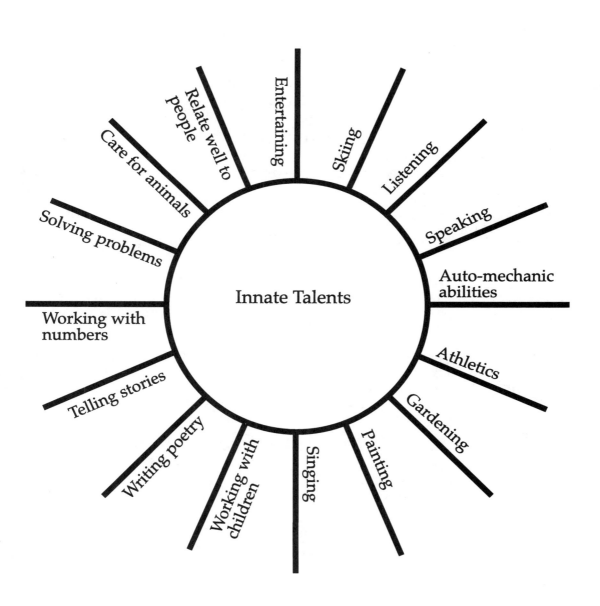

Dance on Broadway
Own a beautiful house on a hill
Hitchhike to Montana
Feel more peaceful
Save the rain forests of the world
Solve the world hunger problem
Own my own boutique
Be famous for my generosity
Start my own company

See the Visionary Dreams Sacred Circle example on page 49.

The Fifth Sacred Circle

The fifth sacred circle is entitled "My Ideal Audience." This particular aspect of rediscovering your soul purpose is often overlooked, but is crucial to the development of your soul purpose. As you consider the combination of your desires, talents, skills and what you love to do, it is essential you stop and ask: In my willingness to serve humanity, what part of humanity do I want to focus on? Not everyone is going to want or need what you have to offer. In fact, some people will be quite negative about how you may want to express yourself. You have to decide who you want to serve and what the needs are of your audience.

When I left my church and decided I wanted to offer my counseling skills, I did an Ideal Audience Sacred Circle. This process showed me that I need to work with people who are self-motivated, dedicated to their spiritual development and who have the ability and desire to pay for my services. I knew I would not be effective with people who wanted to remain victims and stuck in their stuff. Because I do deep spiritual work, I knew that not everyone would want to work with me.

This information was invaluable to me as I created a picture of my ideal client mentality. Based on this, I have developed a thriving counseling practicing working with people who fit my

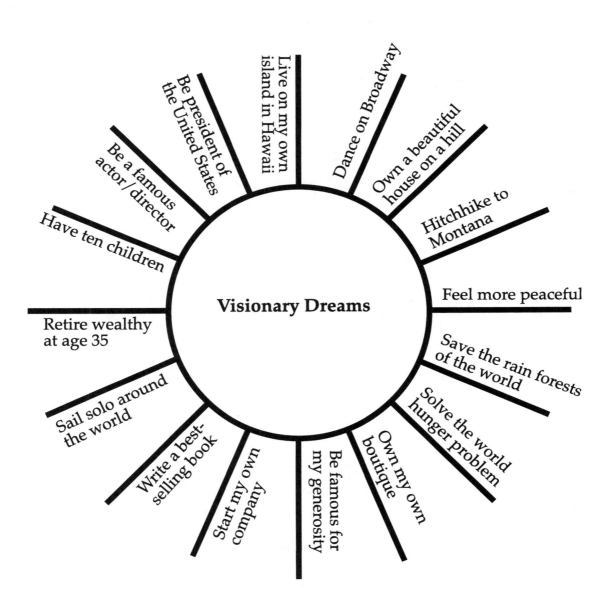

Visionary Dreams

Live on my own island in Hawaii
Dance on Broadway
Own a beautiful house on a hill
Hitchhike to Montana
Feel more peaceful
Save the rain forests of the world
Solve the world hunger problem
Own my own boutique
Be famous for my generosity
Start my own company
Write a best-selling book
Sail solo around the world
Retire wealthy at age 35
Have ten children
Be a famous actor/director
Be president of the United States

ideal audience profile. They benefit from my talents and skills, and in return, I am fulfilled and feel I am expressing my purpose. Describing your ideal audience is an extremely important part of the soul purpose rediscovery process. Some ideas to help you define your ideal audience are:

> they are self-motivated
> they are generous
> they drive Volkswagen cars
> they need computer services
> they are metaphysically-oriented
> they are victims of domestic violence
> they love the outdoors and hiking
> they are writing books and need editing services

See the Ideal Audience Sacred Circle example on page 52.

The Next Step for Your Sacred Circles

Now that you have completed these circles, go back and study each one. Spend a few days adding and deleting items. As you study your sacred circles, you will find that on each one some aspects have more meaning than others. When you feel they are complete, highlight the three most significant entries on each circle.

When you have done this on all of the circles, create a "Soul Purpose Sacred Circle." Transfer the three highlighted entries from all the other Circles onto this one. You now have a complete picture of your most important interests, skills, talents, dreams and audience, and this picture may present a strong indication of what your soul purpose work could be.

When this is complete, put your Soul Purpose Sacred Circle in a place where you will see it regularly, and preferably, meditate on it daily. The subconscious mind responds to programming by repetition and will begin to create this new vision of yourself. As you begin to know yourself better, and own who you are and what you are about, Life will begin to support you in the fulfillment of your soul purpose.

See the Soul Purpose Sacred Circle example on page 53.

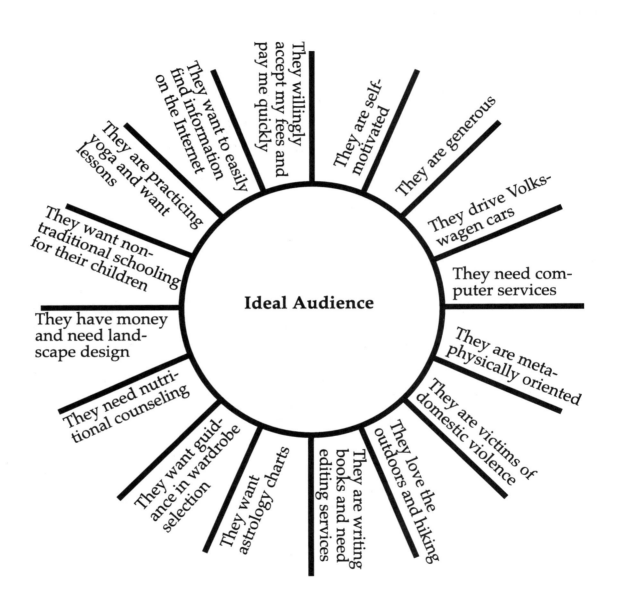

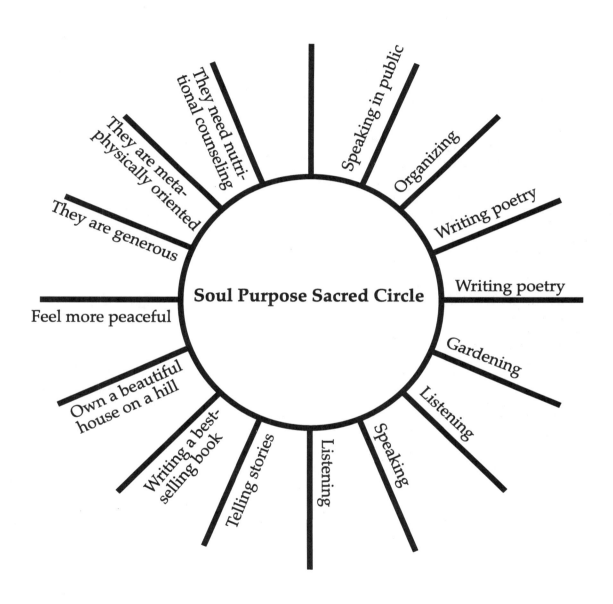

Soul Purpose Sacred Circle

They need nutritional counseling

They are meta-physically oriented

They are generous

Feel more peaceful

Own a beautiful house on a hill

Writing a best-selling book

Telling stories

Listening

Speaking

Listening

Gardening

Writing poetry

Writing poetry

Organizing

Speaking in public

VISION POWER

Harriet's Vision

All the odds were against her. People thought the idea was wild, and logically it did not make sense. Yet deep within her was a feeling she could not ignore. Although she was in her mid-40's, the desire to have a baby would not leave her alone. Harriet's acceptance of her soul purpose was going to take courage, mental discipline and spiritual deepening.

For a long time Harriet had a sense that a special soul was trying to communicate to her, to use her as the vehicle through which it could come from the spiritual to the physical world.

"Even though I am single and alone, and the process of in vitro fertilization can be costly, emotionally wearing, and ineffective, I keep feeling the essence of a beautiful being wanting and needing to come through me," Harriet told me.

Then one morning in 1990, Harriet heard a radio story about a doctor in California who said women could have babies even after age 60! Harriet wrote the doctor and got a quick response: his program was only for married women! Harriet was discouraged but not defeated. Her deep desire, coupled with fierce determination and an awareness of spiritual principles, prepared her for the five-year journey she would have to take to accomplish her goal.

She knew the first step was to re-evaluate how she spent her time. As a 20 year veteran of the teaching profession, her life was busy, but as she scanned her life, she found moments in each day when she could sit quietly and focus, affirm and visualize the realization of her soul purpose.

As time passed, she began to experience a restlessness—as though her creativity needed something to do. With joyful anticipation, she eagerly agreed to create a Soul Purpose Treasure Map: a brightly colored poster board covered with pictures and words that quickly became a beautiful expression of her goal. She filled it with affirmations of health and family well-being, pictures of babies and community activities, and examples of special moments with a partner sharing the joys of parenthood. Feelings of love, prosperity, joy and light emanated from this treasure map. When Harriet proudly unveiled her masterpiece to me, she was beaming brightly.

"This represents exactly what I want to manifest in my life," she said.

"Now, put this in a place in your home," I responded, "where you can study this daily. Remember, the subconscious mind does not know which plane of existence is real . . . and this will help your mind create a pattern for manifesting your desire."

Even in the face of unparalleled odds, Harriet believed in her dream. She was told the process of in vitro fertilization would cost $10,000, *if* she could find a willing doctor. She found the doctor and cashed in her retirement account. Even after many unsuccessful tries at artificial insemination, Harriet refused to give up her dream. Each day, she visualized herself in the future as the mother of a beautiful, healthy child. She saw herself tenderly holding the baby, heard the soft whispers of love she was saying to her newborn, felt the sheer joy flowing through her body as she held her baby. Her future self regularly thanked her present self for the willingness to be focused and disciplined in her pursuit.

At the age of 50, Harriet's dream became a reality and her healthy, beautiful son, Zachary, was born March 29, 1995.

Harriet's story is one of inspiration and courage. She is an example of what happens when we focus our creative energies, open our hearts and minds with the willingness to change, and then say yes to the beckoning of our soul. Does visioning your future really work? Ask Harriet!

Co-Creating our Lives

As humans, we have within us great abilities for manifesting what we want in our lives. *Every physical manifestation on this plane of existence we call planet Earth was first an idea.* Nothing, absolutely nothing, is created by chance. However, if your life at the present time is chaotic or traumatic, don't beat yourself up with this Truth. To awaken to one's creative abilities is the greatest discovery of a lifetime. Use this information to change how you see your life. *A Course in Miracles* reminds us that our greatest tool for change is the ability to alter our perception of the situation, and the best choice is to view our lives with love rather than fear. Knowing that the Universal energy that flows into our lives is orderly and perfect can give us great peace of mind.

When an idea is given focus, imagination and a deep trust in the Universal creative powers, it is made into physical form. Nothing is too big or outrageous for the Great Creator. If you have an idea, and it won't leave you alone, you can be sure that Spirit is trying to get your attention and have the opportunity to co-create with you.

To co-create, we begin by sharpening the finest tool for personal change we have—visualization, the tool of imagining in our minds the desired results. Visualization is not a new concept nor a New Age technique. People have been practicing the science of visualization for thousands of years. Neolithic cave paintings of animals were forms of visualization designed to ensure a successful hunt. Tribal shamans have used the ancient visualization techniques so brilliantly that they have been called the "technicians of the sacred." They used mental pictures of animals and natural objects to connect to the universal knowledge associated with that animal or object in order to gain medicine or power. Similarly, many religious and spiritual leaders throughout human existence have believed that the power of the mind is more valuable than material wealth.

The soul cannot think without pictures.

Aristotle

Imagining can be used for any area you want either to change completely or to expand upon. For example, great athletes such as Sir Roger Bannister, the British athlete who was the first to break the 4-minute mile barrier, attributes his record-breaking 3-minute, 59.4-second mile to the use of his mental powers. He imagined himself winning and breaking the record many times before his record-breaking race of 1954. Bruce Jenner, the 1976 Olympic Decathlon gold medal winner, rehearsed his desired winning outcome for months in his living room.

Successful business people know the power of the mind. Andrew Carnegie, the great 19th century industrialist, and Ray Crock, founder of the MacDonald's restaurant chain, both describe in their autobiographies how extensive use of imagery helped them manifest their goals. Albert Einstein claimed that the theory of relativity came to him during one of his daily dreaming periods. Napoleon Hill, in his book, *The Master Key to Riches*, states, "It is highly significant that the Creator provided man with control over nothing except the power to shape his own thoughts and the privilege of fitting them to any pattern of his choice."

There are countless other historical and modern success stories that claim that harnessing the senses is the first step to manifesting desired outcomes. Whether you want to change your self-esteem, your income, your health, your relationships or your creative expression, the language of the subconscious—imagery—is the most effective tool you have.

There is a natural universal law which we must follow when we live our lives according to our purpose: the Law of Subconscious Activity. As soon as the subconscious mind accepts an idea, it immediately begins to create a pattern that will result in the realization of this idea. It utilizes all the knowledge you have collected, knowledge from the collective unconscious[1], and your conscious and subconscious mental powers to accomplish its goals. Because of this law, it is vitally important that we think about only those ideas we want to experience, and then heartily welcome change into our lives.

VAK to the Future: *a Technique for Enhancing Co-Creation*

The process of focusing our thoughts on what we want to manifest can be strengthened by a technique called *VAK to the Future*[2]. It combines using your representational senses—sight (visual), hearing (auditory), and feeling (kinesthetic), the primary ones, with taste (gustatory) and smell (olfactory) as secondary helpers—in a visualization of your future self experiencing what you want to create.

[1]*Carl Jung, noted Swiss psychologist, developed the idea of the* collective unconscious, *which consists of "those acts and mental patterns shared either by members of a culture or universally by all human beings."*

The Concise Columbia Encyclopedia, Columbia University Press.

[2]*The name,* VAK to the Future, *was created by Robert M. Williams, originator of Psych K™ of Denver, CO.*

Most people are visual thinkers. In fact, 65% of people see a picture when ideas are spoken. Another 20% feel or sense an image and 10% hear images. Whether we are having an external or an internal conversation, most of us instantaneously utilize one or two of our senses in order to comprehend what is being said. Ideally, when we use mental imagery for purposeful self-direction, we will utilize all of the senses.

For example, when you hear the word *orange,* many of you will see in your mind the color orange or a picture of the citrus fruit we call an orange as you are using your visual sense to understand the word. For some of you who are more auditory, you may hear the breaking of the orange peel. Some of you who are kinesthetic, or feeling oriented, will feel the texture of the orange in your hand or the juice flowing down your throat. A few of you will smell an orange and some of you will taste an orange. Some will naturally combine more than one sense in this process of comprehension. Whatever your system, it is your way of using your five senses to comprehend the world.

How to Envision Your Dreams

This exercise is best done with a partner. While you speak about your vision, have your partner write down everything you say. If you don't have a partner, speak into a tape recorder and transcribe it later. The point is to talk freely, without censoring what you say and without stopping to write things down. You will be amazed at what comes out of you.

When we are envisioning, or co-creating what we want, we need to use all of our senses to support our thoughts. To consciously create something in your life, the most effective and powerful place to begin is in your future. Ask yourself what you want to focus on for this exercise: getting a new home, achieving better health, having loving relationships, having a baby, acquiring more money, going on a trip to Hawaii, writing mystery novels, becoming an actress, being at peace—these are some of the

VAK to the Future
A Technique for Enhancing Co-Creation

1)   Decide what your focus or dream is.

2)   Find a quiet space and a partner or a tape recorder to record your vision.

3)   Take a deep breath, relax and see yourself in your future vision—*as if you are living it.*

4)   See yourself living your dream as though you were watching a movie; describe it. Now, visually step into the movie. Describe it. Describe how others see you. Write down these visions.

5)   Hear yourself living your dream; describe it. Describe what others are saying to you. Write the words down.

6)   Feel yourself living your dream; describe it. Describe how others might feel about you. Write these down.

7)   Apply taste and smell sensations to your dream, as appropriate. Describe them. And if possible, include others in these sensations. Write your sensations down.

8)   Lock in your vision by having your future self thank your present self for providing the focus, energy and actions needed to achieve your dream.

subjects my students have chosen.

In your own life right now, you have within you a burning desire to have, do or be something beyond that which is already present. To *desire* something is to be in the flow of life, for desire means *"of the father."* (*Father* in this case means "abundant source.") This refers to the loving energy of unlimited possibilities that surrounds us. The great masters have told us in many different ways, it is "the father's good pleasure to give us what we ask for." In other words, it is the natural impulse of Life to support us in creating what we desire. This is how we are intended to use our creative talents.

Now that you have your focus, close your eyes, take a deep breath and imagine yourself in the future, standing in the center of the experience you would like to have. Just as you could describe your life as it is today, begin to describe your ideal situation and be very detailed!

Let's assume you want to have a new home. Start by describing your new home in general terms. How large is your house? How many rooms does it have and what are they? Where is the house located? Do you see it in a specific city, area or neighborhood? What is the neighborhood like? How close are your neighbors? What kinds of people are they—young suburbanites with children; a mix of ages and ethnic backgrounds in an urban setting; a group of people living on a co-operative farm who all share your spiritual or political beliefs? What is the price of your house?

Once you have created the environment and general aspects of your dream house, begin to use your specific senses to add more details to your vision.

Visual (Seeing)

Imagine you are standing in your new kitchen. Look around you.

What does the kitchen look like? How is the kitchen arranged? Where are the cabinets and appliances? Notice what you have on the walls. What do you see when you look out the windows? What specifically do you see on the counter? What colors do you have in your ideal kitchen? What is the floor made of? How is the kitchen located in relation to the rest of the house? Is it full of people—a gathering place for the family, or is it a gourmet cook's kitchen you share with your mate? Be detailed and specific!

Now move on to the rest of the house. What rooms immediately adjoin the kitchen? What do they look like? How are they used? Walk into your living room? How large is it? Is there a fireplace? If so, what kind? How many windows are there, and what kind of window? What do you see out your windows? What kind and style of furniture is in the living room? What colors are used in this room? What textures do you see; what kinds of art or decorations do you have; and so on. Do this for each room in the house, and for your yard, if you choose to have one.

Now shift your focus to describe how other people see you living in your ideal home. What do they say to you? For example, "They see a big smile on my face." "They see my family playing in the yard." "They see a beautifully-decorated home that displays my collection of antique teddy bears." Be specific!

Visual Exercise for Creating your Vision
Example

What I see as I picture myself in my accomplished vision (be specific and detailed):

❖   My kitchen is large with lots of natural light coming through the windows and skylights.

❖   There is a cooking island in the center of the work area with a rack above to hang pots and pans.

❖　　　The floor is a light wood parquet; the counters are marble and the cabinets are made of light oak and the color scheme is a soft green.

❖　　　The dining room adjoins the kitchen and has an elegant oak dining set which will seat 10 comfortably.

❖　　　The living room opens off of the dining room and is done in soft peach.

❖　　　. . . and so on.

What others see about me as I picture myself in my accomplished vision:

❖　　　My mother sees how proud I am of my beautiful, modern kitchen.

❖　　　My children see me happily maintaining the house.

❖　　　My husband sees me enthusiastically entertaining guests on our beautiful deck in the back yard.

❖　　　. . . and so on.

Auditory (Hearing)

Shift now to what you are hearing yourself say as you stand in your new home. For instance, you might hear yourself excitedly say, "I love my new home! I have great taste! I did it . . . I created what I want! I am so proud of myself!" Can you hear your children playing in the family room? Can you hear your friends having fun as guests in your home? Then describe it. What other sounds can you associate with your ideal home? What sounds come in from outside the home? Are the birds singing; is there a creek nearby; do the trees rustle in the wind?

Now, listen carefully to what others are saying about your new home. "What a beautiful home Susie has." "John and Marie have done such a fabulous job creating what they want." "Did you see Robert's beautiful gourmet kitchen. The colors . . . the design . . . exquisite!"

By using your auditory system, you strengthen your vision and give it more depth.

Auditory Exercise for Creating your Vision
Example

What I say to others as I picture myself in my accomplished vision:

❖ "This kitchen is a dream come true; I have always wanted a modern, beautiful kitchen to cook in."

❖ "Since I've gotten my new house, I'm much more excited about coming home at night to be with my family."

❖ "I am so happy to have you and Bob over; our house just invites others to be part of its wonderful surroundings."

❖ . . . and so on.

What others say to me as I picture myself in my accomplished vision:

❖ "Jody, your kitchen is so fabulous that I am green with envy."

❧   "Honey, you know our life together is much more pleas-
ant since we got the new house. I'm glad we spent the
money."

❧   "Mom, the guys would like to spend the night at our
house. They think our entertainment room is so cool!"

❧   . . . and so on.

Kinesthetic (Feeling)

This approach asks you to focus on how you *feel* in your ideal
situation. What sensations do you feel and where in your body
do you feel them. By focusing on how you feel, you get to choose
what kind of feelings are flowing through you.

For example, in your ideal home, you may feel "warm and
tingling" in your heart area. In order to take this a step deeper,
ask yourself what "warm and tingling" feels like in your body.
Maybe it feels like bubbles flowing from the base of your stom-
ach into your heart. How about rainbow particles bursting forth
from your heart, filtering down into your solar plexus and up
into your shoulders and head? Let your imagination give definition to your feelings.

If you can, describe how others feel about your home. Your
parents may feel pride in your realizing a big dream. How is that
felt by them? Perhaps they might feel pride as a swelling of the
heart. (Remember the expression: "my heart is bursting with
pride"?) Use your imagination.

Kinesthetic Exercise for Creating Your Vision
Example

What sensations I feel when I picture myself in my accomplished vision:

❋ I feel happy and creative when I prepare meals in my new kitchen.

❋ I feel close to my family as we gather in front of the fireplace and eat popcorn.

❋ I feel so proud when visitors come over and admire the art work we have in our home.

❋ . . . and so on.

What sensations others feel when they are in my presence as I picture myself in my accomplished vision:

❋ John's parents feel pride as they see what a wonderful home we've built.

❋ My wife's friends feel happy when they are invited over for a gathering.

❋ My children's friends feel comfortable and safe when they play in our house or yard.

❋ . . . and so on.

Gustatory (Taste)

Imagine now that you are sitting at your dining room table. On the table is spread your favorite meal. As you look at the plates of food, *see* how beautifully arranged they are. *Hear* the sounds of people enjoying a meal together. Notice how you *feel*. And now, pick up the fork and begin to eat. As you put your favorite food in your mouth, *taste* it. How does it taste? Spicy? Salty? Sweet? What is the texture of the food on your tongue?

What other taste-related sensations can you associate with your new home? Do you have certain foods that are associated with special occasions, like birthdays or holidays? Can you envision sharing food with friends and family? Whatever you can imagine will help to strengthen your vision.

Gustatory Exercise for Creating Your Vision
Example

What I taste as I picture myself in my accomplished vision:

❖ I taste a delicious Thanksgiving dinner as my entire family gathers together in our house for the holiday.

❖ I taste the pretzels, pizza and beer as we watch the football playoffs with friends.

❖ I taste my son's birthday cake as we celebrate this event with his friends.

❖ . . . and so on.

What others taste as they are in my presence as I picture myself in my accomplished vision:

❖ My family tastes the delicious Thanksgiving dinner that I

have lovingly prepared: the turkey, stuffing, mashed potatoes, squash, salad, pumpkin and mince pies, the wine and coffee.

❖ Our friends taste the grilled hamburgers and fixings we have prepared on our barbecue and eat on the deck on a hot summer evening.

❖ . . . and so on.

Olfactory (Smell)

What smells can you associate with the meal you have just tasted? Can you see yourself baking cookies in your kitchen? Then *smell* them. Can you see yourself watching TV with popcorn and soda in your lap? Then smell the popcorn and the soda.

What else besides food can you smell in your house? Walk into your family or living room and sit down. Close your eyes, relax, and begin to smell the flowers you have in the vase on your bookshelf. Do you pick up a hint of the lemon oil used to polish your furniture? If you or a member of your family has a hobby, what smells are associated with that? For example, if you paint with oils, smell the turpentine and oil paint. If someone is a woodworker, smell the scent of the different woods, the glue, the sawdust or the paint. Again, whatever you can imagine will help to strengthen your vision.

Olfactory Exercise for Creating Your Vision
Example

What I smell as I picture myself in my accomplished vision:

❊ I smell the gardenias on the coffee table in the living room.

❊ I smell the turpentine and oil paints my daughter uses when she paints in the family room.

❊ I smell the odor of shoe polish as my husband prepares for our evening out.

❊ . . . and so on.

What others smell as they are in my presence as I picture myself in my accomplished vision:

❊ Visitors smell the gardenias in the living room.

❊ My husband smells the dinner cooking when he comes home from work.

❊ My children smell the irresistible odor of popcorn as we get ready to watch a video on Sunday night.

❊ . . . and so on.

Locking in Your Vision

Take another deep breath now, and as you see, hear, feel, taste and smell your ideal vision as your future self experiences it, give thanks to the current you—the you that is now in your past—that accepted this vision and gave the time, energy and focus to bring this dream into physical form. This past you deserves to be acknowledged. Thank yourself.

This acknowledgment by your future self of your present self locks in your vision by putting a boundary on it. The reason this is important is because you will immediately begin to think about other things, and you don't want those thoughts to merge with your vision—to contaminate it. It is essential that you complete the process. The thanking of your current self by your future self is a completion of your vision—an exclamation point at the end of your sentence.

There is one other rule to this process and it is very important. Your job is to determine what you want, not how it is going to unfold. When we get clear on what it is we want to accept into our lives, our job is to *passionate the vision*—give it depth, meaning and focus. Do not try to figure out how your vision is going to be happen. Do not allow yourself to think about all the reasons why it can't be. When we signal to the Universe that we are serious about manifesting our desires, it guides us to the right people, places and things that will help us create what we want. As we focus on what we want, we become magnets that attract all we need to accomplish our desires. Our human perception is limited, and we must leave the *how* to the Great Creator who has the full picture of our process and our life purpose. The essential quality for this process is trust. Trust that what is unseen in your life is real. It exists. Believe not only that you deserve to have the life you want, but that you trust the Great Creator to support you.

Genius Treasure Mapping

After you've spent some time focusing on your Soul Purpose Sacred Circle (Chapter 3), it is time to create a Genius Treasure Map. Making a Genius Treasure Map is fun and powerful. It is fun because your inner child has an opportunity to express itself, and it is powerful because it is a physical representation of your desired manifestations. Your subconscious mind cannot distinguish between what is thought and what has actually been manifested. By creating a Genius Treasure Map, which includes pictures or symbols of what you want to manifest in your life, you trick your subconscious into acting like your wishes are already reality and it begins to adjust your behavior to match the reality. As you behave *as if* these wishes are already real, you help to draw to you those people, ideas and opportunities needed to create your wishes in physical form.

To create a Genius Treasure Map, you will need the following supplies:

> a large colored poster board
> a picture of something that reminds you of your
>   spirituality
> magazines
> affirmations
> colored pens
> glue
> pictures of yourself
> a statement to be placed somewhere on your map that
>   reads, "This or Something Better."

Transformation is the ability and willingness to live beyond your form.

Wayne Dyer

To begin, glue your spiritual symbol in the center of the board to remind you of your connection to the Great Creator which is the source of your genius creativity. You can use the entire map to represent one desire or focus, or you can divide the map into several quadrants to represent several desires. Some people choose to divide the map into four quadrants to represent the four basic areas of our lives: health, prosperity, relationships and creativity. Using colored pictures from magazines, affirmations, drawings that you make, pictures of yourself, and other things, paste items on your board that represent your ideal, realized desires.

For example, if your desire is improved health, you might choose to include pictures of people who are physically fit and actively participating in sports or other physical activities. You might include pictures of healthy food, vitamins or other such things that remind you to make better eating choices. You might include a picture of a health club, an exercise class, a yoga class, a piece of exercise equipment for the home, or some other representation of your desire to incorporate regular exercise in your life. If you want to lose weight, you might include your ideal weight and dress or pant size.

Don't be restricted by these suggestions. Whatever is meaningful to you is valid. The items you include do not have to be understandable to others as long as they are to you. Also, the more vivid and colorful your Genius Treasure Map is, the greater the impact on your subconscious mind.

Warning*: Do not include pictures or representations of what you don't want.* If you need to quit smoking, then include an affirmation that says, "I am easily and comfortably smoke-free." Your subconscious mind is very literal and does not understand subtleties. Whatever you picture must be the positive state of what you want, not the negative state you want to eliminate.

Be sure to include the words "This or something better" on you Genius Treasure Map. You cannot see the whole picture, whereas the Great Creator can. You may be asking for a small piece of pie when the Universe is willing and able to provide you the whole pie! This affirmation allows the Universe to improve on your own personal vision.

When you have completed your map, put it in a place where you can look at it, study it and embody it daily. Then watch how the Universe supports you. You will begin to attract people, ideas and opportunities into your life that will help and support you in manifesting your desires. Situations will occur that will directly support your move toward manifesting your soul purpose. What you focus on expands. The more you focus on your genius self, the sooner you become it.

An Experience with Genius Treasure Mapping

When I was in ministerial school in the mid 1980's, I met a man who had a fascinating experience using Genius Treasure Mapping. He was a true believer in this process. This man had a deep desire to go to Hawaii and a shallow pocket of money, so he created a Genius Treasure Map representing this desire. He cut out all kinds of pictures of beaches, waterfalls, leis, flowers, and other Hawaiian themes. He typed out many different positive affirmations and found his spiritual picture. Most important, he cut out pictures of men in Hawaiian settings and substituted pictures of his head on their bodies. He then glued everything onto a white board. When completed, he proudly placed his Genius Treasure Map on the wall of his bathroom so he would be sure to study it every day.

About this time, our church was conducting a fund-raiser with a lottery for a trip to Hawaii. There was much excitement for six weeks. Finally the day came for our minister to draw the winning ticket. You guessed it! My friend won. He was very proud of his accomplishment and excited about his upcoming trip.

When he returned, however, he had quite an experience to relate. Hawaii is usually known for its sunshine, but, when it rains, it's a deluge! My friend said he had never seen so much rain. In fact, not only had it rained incredibly hard, he never once saw the sun! He spent most of time enjoying his accomplishment inside a hotel room.

When he looked afterward at his Genius Treasure Map, he saw that he had created 90% of his map using black and white pictures! Well, his subconscious mind had given him what he asked for. His whole trip had happened in shades of gray! Fortunately, he saw the humor in this lesson in the literalness of the subconscious mind.

Letter of Legacy

As a minister, I have the privilege of serving people at peak moments in their lives: weddings, funerals, christenings, and other memorable events. Most weddings, although not all, are joyful occasions. Oddly enough, so are many funerals. While funerals are a time of sadness and grief, they can also be joyful when people truly celebrate the life of the departed. This usually occurs when people understand the truth that life is eternal, and that the loved one has not ceased to exist but has only shed a body no longer needed. While the process of leaving one's body looks and feels like an ending to those of us left behind, it is indeed a new beginning somewhere beyond our ordinary reality.

If you were told you had one day to live . . . who would you want to call, what would you say to them . . . and why are you waiting.

Steven Levine

After my first funeral service, I began to have mystical experiences. As I lead people through the prayers, eulogies and meditations, I am acutely aware that the essence of the person about whom we are speaking is present at the service! Because I know they are part of the funeral service, it is my desire to acknowledge and honor the soul qualities of these people accurately and authentically. To be able to do this, I like to work with the person before he or she makes the transition.

Working with people who are about to transition has taught me that planning your own eulogy is a very powerful experience. To be able to tell another how you want to be remembered after you transition out of this life allows you to put your life in perspective, and to emphasize those things in your life that are most meaningful for you. No one can describe you as well as you can. And no one else knows the true context of the struggles and successes of your life.

The Letter of Legacy exercise gives you the chance to write your eulogy now but to set it in the indefinite future. That way, you can create the life you want to have lived by the time you really do transition. In other words, create your present-day reality from the future, using the past as a back-drop. This process asks you to take charge of your life and take responsibility for creating the legacy you wish to leave behind.

This exercise is best done with a friend. Writing the Letter of Legacy may trigger some intense emotions. Make this okay. Emotion is just energy moving through our bodies, and allowing the emotion to move through can be very healing. Allow your friend to support you by writing down the information as you tell it. This will keep you from editing as you think. You will be surprised at what comes up. This exercise, if done with complete honesty, can reveal your hidden desires and yet-to-be-manifested accomplishments.

Before you begin writing, take a deep breath, close your eyes and travel in time into the future to the moment just after your soul has transitioned when you are looking back on the lifetime you've just completed. Spend a few minutes asking yourself:

1.   How do I want my life to be remembered?

2.   What were the qualities I want others to remember about me?

3.   What were my greatest accomplishments?

4.   . . . and most important, what were my greatest loves?

When you are ready, write your Letter of Legacy

This process alone has caused major shifts not only in my own life, but for many of my clients and students. It causes one to have a deep reverence for everyday living and to realize the preciousness of the gift of life. It also generates a sense of responsibility towards one's life. We are not victims of circumstances. Indeed, we are the creators of our circumstances and no moment exists when we do not have choice. The Letter of Legacy is designed to remind us of this.

Letter of Legacy

We are here today to honor and celebrate the life of someone near and dear to us, the life of Jane Doe (use your name).

❖ Jane has touched all our lives with love and joy. Her greatest gift to each of us is that she is an example of a fully-actualized human being who has lived life passionately. She knew her soul purpose, and with joy and discipline, used her genius self to create a life of wonderment, prosperity, health, harmony and love.

❖ The qualities that describe Jane best are:
loving
joyful - loved to laugh
prosperous
generous
talented (describe in depth)
adventuresome

❖ Jane had many accomplishments. Some of them are:
Made a successful solo climb of Mt. Everest
Fought off three Anaconda snake attacks in
the jungles of the Amazon
Wrote four best-selling adventure books
Sang in Carnegie Hall

❖ Jane led a life of real passion. Her greatest loves were:
Jeremy, her husband
Rex, her beloved Irish Setter
Soft, ripe, sweet-smelling mangos
Traveling in a hot air balloon
Most of all, she loved her Aunt Gertrude

And so it is with honor and love that we acknowledge <u>Jane Doe</u>. We know that her life has contributed to the great tapestry of eternal life, and that her greatest gift has been her existence. We recognize that the memories of <u>Jane</u> are her greatest legacy to we who remain behind.

And for this blessed life, which touched us individually and collectively, we give thanks. And so it is . . .

ACTION POWER

The Flight of the Eagle

It was a cool, rainy Saturday afternoon. I was curled up on my soft, white living room couch in front of the fire. My lemon herbal tea steaming, my eyes closed, I breathed with the melodious sounds of Enya singing, ". . . sail away, sail away . . . ." I was reveling in this rare, quiet moment of relaxation. Slowly I felt myself shift from a time-and-space reality to an altered state of quiescent consciousness. I was reminded of one of my favorite quotes: "How beautiful it is to do nothing and then rest afterwards." I said a silent prayer of thanks for my hour to do nothing and sank into the peacefulness of the moment.

Suddenly, I was jolted back to reality. My heart began to pound and my hands sweat as I became alert and awake. I heard my eleven-year-old son Corey walk in and could immediately feel his need to talk. I intuitively knew my hour of doing nothing had shrunk to five minutes.

"Mom, there is something I need to tell you and don't get mad" he said as he sat down on the edge of the couch. "I need you to know that I am smoking and think I am addicted."

BOOM! There went my peace and quiet. A panicked, reactive part of me started screaming inside: *YOU ARE DOING WHAT? You are only eleven years old! Smoking . . . anything but smoking! Not only are you forbidden to smoke again, but you are grounded for the next 25½ years!*

Fortunately, a more conscious and responsive part of me gently thought, "Hmm. This is interesting—I started smoking at age eleven. Honor this boy and his process."

I sat up, put my arm around him and said, "You know, I used to smoke. In fact, I smoked 2 to 3 packs of Marlboro cigarettes a day for 17 years. I quit four years before you were born. What kind are you smoking?"

"What a coincidence, Mom! I smoke Marlboros, too," he grinned.

My heart sank! All my feelings of being a negligent, absent mother rose to my consciousness. This child was not getting his needs met. How did I know? I started smoking at age eleven because my needs were not being met.

The truth was that I was extremely out of balance, working 10 to 15 hours a day, 6 days a week. The ministry can be very demanding and I was allowing the needs of others to come before the needs of my family. This imbalance in my life was creating a dark and looming dysfunction. But what was causing the greatest imbalance in my life was the lack of joy and purpose in my work. Living one's soul purpose brings balance and centeredness into one's life, and I was definitely *not* living my soul purpose! When we are living our soul purpose, the ecology of our entire life, including family, community and—most importantly—self, is clean and pure.

A major aspect of soul purpose is living a life of balance— balance of time, energy and focus. The dance of balance is an ever-flowing process around a center within us, which I call the *light center*. It is the source of our inner wisdom. It guides and directs us into our well-being, leading us away from our compulsions, and nudging us to consciously step into the light of our soul purpose and live authentic lives.

For many people, getting off center—out of balance—causes them enough pain that they listen to their inner voice and do what is necessary to get back into balance. Because of my high tolerance for pain, it sometimes takes a whack from a golden 2-by-4 to get me to wake up.

The day Corey shared his smoking habit with me was just such a wake-up call. I knew that to forbid my beautiful son to smoke would impede his developmental process, and it wouldn't have worked anyway. He would only have used his creative talents to find ways to get around this rule. But I had to set some boundaries.

"Okay, here's the deal, Bud," one of my terms of endearment for him, "you can continue to smoke but not at home or church. Period."

"Oh, real nice, Mom, and why not?" he responded with a huge sigh of frustration.

"Because it doesn't feel right to me. As a family, we're trying to keep our house and yard environment clean and pure, and the same goes for the church. These are not places to practice destructive habits."

As the weeks passed, I kept a closer check on the ecology of my life. Work was still demanding, especially because I was doing a job that was no longer supporting my soul purpose, but I was much more present with my family.

Two months after our smoking conversation, Corey came to me again. "Mom," he said brightly, "I want you to know I've quit smoking, but I have two cigarettes left and I'd like to do a celebration ritual with you." I stood there breathless, with tears welling up in my eyes.

"You would?" I said softly. "I would be honored. Okay, we've both been very busy, so you skip school on Wednesday and I'll skip work, and we'll go to the beach and create a celebration ceremony. We'll spend the whole day there."

His eyes lit up. An adventure in honor of him was in the making.

And so on Wednesday morning, Corey, Yuki—our fluffy, white dog—and I went to the beach. As we approached Cannon Beach on the Oregon Coast, it was somewhere between drizzling and raining, but we had a mission to fulfill and nothing was going to stop us.

As the three of us walked out on the soft, golden brown sand, I said to myself, "Take this all in, Jody. It could be one of the most precious moments of your life." As I listened to the melodious sounds of the waves, I watched my son and his dog run down the beach and felt truly blessed.

After walking the beach for about an hour, we found a large sand dune that would block the wind. Yuki curled up behind Corey as if to offer him a special kind of support. After digging a deep hole in the sand, Corey brought out the red Marlboro box with the two remaining cigarettes, and tore apart the box and crushed the cigarettes into small pieces. We both wanted every bit of tobacco to be transformed into ashes.

I bent over to ceremoniously ignite the pile and protected the burning match with our cupped hands. As the fire took hold, we clasped our hands together and bowed our heads.

"Let's take a deep breath, Bud, and each of us give thanks to the curiosity that caused both of us to start smoking, and recognize that the fire which is transforming the poisonous cigarettes to ashes is symbolic of letting go of our destructive ways of dishonoring our bodies—the temples of our souls. Let us give thanks for our willingness to change our habits and ways of being. We also acknowledge that our lives are an ever-unfolding process, and as we grow in awareness, we will treat ourselves more lovingly and respectfully."

I looked into Corey's eyes and whispered, "I'm so proud to be your mom." And he replied, "I'm so grateful to be your son." The moment was sacred: we sighed, cried and laughed. Then we buried the ashes, making sure everything was in its place.

"Hey, Corey Mac," I said with a twinkle in my eye, "In the animal kingdom, there are animals that have similar energy to our own. If you could be an animal, what would you be?" Without a moment's hesitation, he said, "An eagle!"

"Yes, yes, yes!" I shouted. "Two months ago my son was a smoker. Now he is an eagle!"

His answer created another mission for us, and for the next four hours, we searched the boutiques and shops lining the main road of this small, ocean town looking for a symbol of his eagle energy.

Just as the stores were closing, we found what we were looking for. As we entered a brass and antique shop, we noticed a dust-covered brass eagle. Its majestic wings were spread as if in mid-flight.

We both squealed with delight. "That's it," exclaimed Corey. "That's it!"

That day will remain forever sacred to both of us. Taking the time to be with loved ones; co-creating a ceremony that acknowledges growth and love is one of the greatest gifts we can give to ourselves. This particular day was a turning point in my life. While driving home and reviewing the events of the day, I vowed to look ruthlessly at the priorities in my life.

Until that day, my priorities had been causing me and my family great imbalance and hardship. I was physically, emotionally and spiritually exhausted. I was not setting my priorities with my soul purpose in mind. My first priority was my work; my second, my relationship with the Great Creator; my third, my family and friends. If and only if there was time left over, I became the fourth priority. But this particular day changed my life. My awareness shifted which resulted in a shift in my priorities. From that day forward, my relationship with the Abundant Universe became my number one focus. Then ME! Then my family and friends, and finally, my work.

What are your priorities? Where is the focus of your spiritual life? How important is your work and does it take priority over all other creative expressions in your life? If you are experiencing a fair amount of drama, trauma and chaos, it is because you are not making yourself the number one priority of your life.

Flushing Out the Toxins in Our Lives

In the close of the 20th century, we live on a generally degraded planet. Most of us are aware of the bigger global environmental problems: dirty air and water; poisons in our food chain; ozone depletion; chemical contamination; toxic waste dumps; oil spills;

crime, poverty and over-crowding in the cities; loss of species; destruction of the rain forest. But our environment is also personal—how we treat the temple of our soul. Our physical bodies are a reflection of the bigger picture. What we eat, what we wear, where and how we work, who we associate with, the thoughts we think—these constitute our personal environment. And for many of us, our personal environment is unhealthy.

Toxins are those things that cause a negative chemical and/or vibrational effect in our lives which can be poisonous to our physical bodies and damaging to our souls. The foods we eat, the materials we use in our homes and in our clothing, our work environment—all have a chemical effect on our physical body, which in turn influences our emotional and spiritual well-being.

There are four major categories of possible toxicity in our everyday lives: food, time, people and negative thinking. To live a life directed by our soul purpose, we must make a ruthless inventory of the toxins in our lives and begin to make choices to eliminate them.

Toxic Food

Nutritionists are fond of reminding us that "you are what you eat." Food, and other substances we ingest, have an immediate and direct influence on our bodies. We are a walking chemical factory. Whatever we put into our bodies is converted to chemicals and enters our bloodstream and eventually our brains. The liver is the main organ that detoxifies whatever is harmful to the body, but there is a limit to how much it can handle. When we don't fuel our bodies properly, then we pay the price in ill health and a lessened state of functioning, and then we wonder why we feel tired, ineffective and resentful.

A race-car driver who wanted to win the Indy 500 would put only the finest gasoline and oil into his car. He would make sure that the engine was maintained regularly and that it was tuned to perform at its peak capabilities. If we want to go for our gold, which is to fully express our soul purpose, then we must fuel and maintain our bodies as meticulously as a race-car driver would his racing car.

The American diet, our fuel, is generally quite toxic. According to the *Chicago Tribune,* the top-ten grocery store products sold in American today are:

1. Marlboro Cigarettes
2. Classic Coke
3. Pepsi Cola
4. Kraft Cheese (highly processed, lots of chemicals)
5. Diet Coke
6. Campbell's Soup (lots of salt)
7. Budweiser Beer
8. Tide Detergent
9. Folgers Coffee
10. Winston Cigarettes

These are not the substances of champions. The average American is overweight, out-of-shape and chronically tired in spite of the popularity of health clubs and low-fat foods. It is time we got into immediate recovery. In order to fully express your soul purpose, you need a healthy body as a vehicle of expression. Begin today to make better choices in what you put into your body.

Since we are all physically different, I will share only the barest outline of my health plan: (1) eliminate or severely limit your intake of the known poisons: alcohol, tobacco, drugs, highly processed foods, chemical additives, junk foods. (2) Cleanse your body regularly by drinking pure water and herbal teas; (3) choose a balanced selection of wholesome foods to eat; and (4) exercise regularly. There are many different philosophies about what foods to eat, when and in what combination, how much to exercise and what kinds of exercise are best. Find a knowledgeable health care professional to help you make wise decisions. Educate yourself and make your choices based on your needs and lifestyle. Begin today to treat your body as the sacred machine that is your only and best tool for expressing your soul purpose.

Toxic Time-wasters

Time is of the essence—quite literally. Time is not a substance but a human measurement which exists only in this reality we call Earth. Whenever I ask my students what is the one thing you need more of in your life, I hear a unanimous answer: "More time!" You cannot hold onto time, stop time, push time or have more time. While we can measure time on a clock or by a calendar, in truth, there is no such thing as the past or the future. There is only the *now*.

I was having a conversation with my two boys one night. We were talking about this very thing. They were adamant that there is such a thing as the future and the past. I kept saying, "only in mind. Physically, you cannot stand in the past, nor can you stand in the future." They continued to argue.

I said, "Go ahead and raise your arm in the future."

As Cam raised his arm, I smiled and said, "Come on now, raise your arm in the future. You keep raising your arm in the present."

Corey eagerly spoke up and said, "I'll raise my hand in the past." We laughed. As hard as he tried, every time he raised his hand in the past, it became the present.

So when I hear from my clients and students, "I need more time," what they are really saying is, "I don't know how to manage my time in the moment." Most of us are guilty of spending time doing things we don't want to do, or being with people we'd really rather not be with. How do you feel when this

Einstein realized that time and space are . . . products of our five senses; . . . Yet Einstein and his colleagues were able to remove this mask of appearances . . . . The old space-time model was smashed, replaced by a timeless flowing field of constant transformation.

Deepak Chopra,
Ageless Body,
Timeless Mind.

happens? Frustrated? Mad at yourself? Badly used by others? These negative feelings are a sign that we are poisoning our system. When we misuse our time this way, they become *toxic time wasters.*

According to *USA Today (April 13, 1989),* it would take a person about 42 hours a day to include all you should in your life.

Exercise	½ hr.
Personal grooming	45 min.
Time with children	4 hrs.
Reading newspapers	45 min.
Pets	50 min.
Housekeeping/chores	½ hrs.
Work	7-10+ hrs.
Commuting	1½ hrs.
Errands	up to 2 hrs.
Grocery shopping (men)	17.88 min.
(women)	22.25 min.
Cooking, eating dinner	1 hr.
Entertaining	1 hr.
Dental care	18 min.
Sex/intimacy	50 min.
General time with spouse	6 hrs.
Volunteering	½ hr.
Time with plants	10 min.
Time for you	1 hr.
Reading a book	15 min.
Spiritual development	15 min.
Sleep	7½ hrs.
Total:	about 42 hours.

A soul-purposed person is not interested in time management. It is too limiting. A soul-purposed person is interested in *purpose management.* When you focus on purpose rather than time, your priorities become clear. If your purpose is to lead a balanced, joy-filled, harmonious life, then you will become ruthless in how you use your time and how you expend your creative energies. You will make decisions based on your purpose and not your available time.

Purpose management demands that we put ourselves as the first priority in our lives. Purpose management allows us to see clearly where we are giving our time and energy away, and where we must make changes. This does not mean I am advocating selfishness or a lack of compassion for others' needs. I am saying that when you use your time in pursuit of your soul purpose, in pursuit of what is important to you, you will make choices that are good for your body and spirit, and not feed your dysfunctions. Co-dependent issues need to be addressed if you care more about other people than you do yourself.

If your purpose is to just make it through the day, make enough money for the month, or get that two week vacation each year, then you will want to improve your time management. This is useful if you have a tendency to be scattered, co-dependent, or so detailed in your focus your forget to notice the big picture. Scattered energies need to be harnessed in order for you to function effectively throughout the day. There are 1,440 minutes in a 24-hour period. You choose, minute by minute, breath by breath, how to express your creative talents and what kind of environment you live in.

Toxic People

One of the greatest challenges of saying yes to our soul purpose is that we begin to notice the dysfunctional, or toxic, elements in our lives. As our awareness increases, our tolerance decreases. This is especially true with people. As we become more self-aware, we become sensitive to the people in our lives whose energies are poisonous, the *energy depleters*. The most obvious energy depleters are those people who are negative and sarcastic. These people are very poisonous to all they contact. While it is compassionate to understand that these people are negative and sarcastic because they are wounded, their way of being can negatively affect all those around them.

As you move into the energy field of your soul purpose and your sensitivity increases, so does your ability to choose differently. You begin to feel restless and irritated with the nay-sayers, the person who only has negative comments about others, the person who constantly puts down him/herself or others. You start to notice how you feel around certain negative people—how they poison the atmosphere around them.

Choosing to spend less time with an energy depleter is not always easy, especially if the person is a family member. And yet, the influence of toxic people in our lives can be debilitating. They can steal our self-esteem, sap our positive energy, pull our focus off of our goals and depress us.

To live the impulse of our soul purpose demands that we consciously and ruthlessly choose the people with which we surround ourselves. People have a direct and powerful impact on our energy field. The awareness of this allows us to make positive and life-enhancing decisions that further us in the expressing of our soul purpose.

Negative Thinking

The most toxic form of pollution in our lives is negative thinking. The vibrational effect our thoughts have on our lives is more powerful than an earthquake. Why? Because every thought we have has the potential of manifesting itself into our reality. Negative thinking is poisonous—even dangerous to our survival. Shifting from negative to positive thinking is easy to learn, but not always simple to achieve.

As we look out across the sea of humanity, we acknowledge a multitude of serious problems and challenges. Human existence is often painful and confusing. But what we focus on expands. If we focus on the drama, trauma and chaos of human living, we create more of it. We are thinking horizontally. We see one situation, and immediately look around to find other similar situations, which reinforces our opinion about the first situation. As a soul-purposed person, we must become vertical thinkers. We must rise above the situation in order to see the causes and the possible solutions. To find a solution, to create our lives from a position of positive power, we must go to a higher level of awareness with our minds in order to allow new energy to flow into the situation. The simple technique of saying to yourself over and over again in the midst of a crisis, ". . . something good is trying to happen here . . . ," is very powerful. Then begin to look for the pearl and it will be revealed. Remember, what you focus on expands. No solution is ever found at the level of the problem.

Harnessing negative thinking is one of the most powerful toxic releasers you can do for yourself. Positive thoughts affect you physically, mentally and spiritually. As you choose to think from the well-being of your life—and not from the drama, trauma and chaos—your soul purpose begins to emerge. You feel more prosperous, healthy, loving and joy-filled, and your life will begin to reflect it. The choice is yours.

Boundary Busters

Boundary Busters are those elements in our lives that we say yes to when we really want to say no. Setting boundaries is essential for eliminating the toxins in our lives, and for reinforcing our self-awareness. They create a clearly defined sense of self, a sense of identity.

According to Dr. Jan Lisonbee, expert on boundary issues, ". . . a boundary is a system of limit setting which allows us to maintain a sense of self." The metaphor Dr. Lisonbee uses to define a boundary is a cell.

If you take a cell and look at the wall and its function, you will see that a healthy wall is semi-permeable, allowing fluid to pass both ways. In its healthy state, it will keep out unhealthy chemicals and let in health producing substances. A healthy boundary protects appropriately and relaxes appropriately. It is fluid but discriminating.

In order to create healthy boundaries, we need to use both our masculine (yang) energies and our feminine (yin) energies. Our yang, or masculine, energies are the logical, the intellectual, the protective/aggressive part. It is the part of ourselves that determines our separateness, our uniqueness from others. Our yin, or feminine, energies are the intuitive, the non-logical, the creative, the receptive/nurturing part. This part allows for influence by and interaction with others.

Our unique pattern of establishing—or failing to establish—boundaries is determined in early childhood. One of the greatest destroyers of the development of our soul purpose is inappropriate boundaries. There are two primary boundary busters. The first is the over-developed yang influence. Characteristic of this type of person is rigidly fixed boundaries. He or she may feel superior but it is usually a mask for the true feelings of being alone, abandoned or being badly used. Their mental viewpoint and non-verbal language says to others, "I am not available to fully participate in human living . . . I might have to be too vulnerable." These people are attached to hierarchy and control, and become rigid and protective of themselves. They are distrustful of others. They are the *takers* of humanity.

The characteristic of the other boundary buster is the over-developed yin type who has a poorly-developed sense of self and too-permeable boundaries. These people often give too much of themselves and let others use them. They exude victim energy, feel less worthy than others and resentful of their abusers. An over-developed yin personality feels tired, angry, alone, hates him/herself, and is passively aggressive. These are the *door-mats* of society.

The final piece for flushing out the toxins in our lives as we step into our soul purpose is learning to set healthy personal boundaries. This means we must learn to say yes when we mean yes and no when we mean no. When asked the number one rule for developing healthy boundaries, Dr. Lisonbee replied, "Know yourself and BE it. It takes more than just knowing yourself, you have to BE yourself and live it."

To help you learn to set healthy boundaries, focus on the following six guidelines:

❖   *Be aware of yourself.*

Become aware of your values, your interests, your needs and your goals.

❖   *Listen to your heart.*

Within you are the answers to any challenge or situation you may face. Learn how to listen to your intuition, that small, quiet voice within you, and it will help you navigate through the perils of life.

❖   *Use your intellectual powers.*

When we learn to blend our intellectual abilities with our intuition, we create a much stronger personal force as our intellectual abilities are harnessed to our personal values and goals.

❖   *Have courage.*

Sometimes on our path to purpose, we have to make decisions and take actions that do not logically make sense, or go against the norm. It takes courage to walk to the edge of our reality and step off into the unknown.

❖ *Trust in the rightness of what you are undertaking.*

When we make known our authentic needs, especially when this practice is new to us, we need to trust that whatever the reaction is from people is perfect. As we begin to set new boundaries, this becomes unsettling to others and they may react in undesirable ways. Trust becomes the foundation that allows us to proceed in establishing new boundaries.

❖ *Create a support system for yourself.*

We need to find loving family and friends who will listen to us, support us, but when it is appropriate, stop us and ask what different choices we could make. People who love us enough to tell us the truth and keep us accountable are essential to boundary development. We can also find support in motivational books, tapes and support groups.

Foundations

Whenever we go from one level of expressing our soul purpose genius to another in our lives, we open ourselves up to major changes and shake-ups. There will be moments of elation and moments of depression. There will be times when we feel that we are on top of the world, everything is running smoothly and life is grand—all channels of creative energy are open and flowing; and then, boom! In a moment's notice, our life feels like it has been turned upside down. We feel confused, tired, broken, and very much alone.

It is at times like this that having a *foundational support system* is essential. Foundations keep you going forward when you are sure your life is going backwards, and keep you buoyed up when you are convinced you are drowning. Foundations inspire, motivate and remind you how loved and supported by the Universe you truly are.

What is a foundational support system? It is made up of people you admire, ideas which inspire and motivate you, and personal friends who can give you support when things get tough. Your foundational support system has five components:

1. A list of the three people you most admire and why.
2. A list of three reasons why you should continue when you want to give up.
3. A list of three persons you can call on, who really believe in you, when you stop believing in yourself.
4. A list of three affirmations that inspire you.
5. Spiritual communities and support groups.

Developing a foundational support system assists us in igniting our courage and accepting more love in our lives.

Three People I Most Admire and Why

Through the ages there have been people who have expressed their highest levels of genius soul expression. In spite of enormous obstacles, these people have persevered and stayed true to the impulses of their souls. Their lives have become an inspiration to others to attain a greater level of soul purpose expression. Some examples are:

❋ Helen Keller, who learned to communicate great wisdom even though she was deaf and blind

❖   Victor Frankl, who survived the atrocities of the Nazi concentration camps to find the true expression of his worth, which he has brilliantly shared with the rest of the world

❖   Ken Montgomery, a member of my former church, who at the youthful age of 85, with many physical challenges, has gone back to college to earn his masters degree.

There are people in your history books; there are modern day mystics, and there are ordinary people in your own life who can inspire you to keep your head up, your heart open and your soul awake.

See the sample below and write down the three people you most admire and why.

Foundation 1
"Three People I Admire and Why"
Example

Person #1: <u>Beatrice Grazziola</u>

I am inspired by <u>my grandmother, Beatrice Grazziola</u> because she came over to the United States from Italy by herself at the age of 15 to join her uncle and aunt in eastern Washington. She came because her family was very poor and had lots of children, and she wanted a chance to go beyond elementary school, which was all that was available in her small Sicilian village.

She worked for her uncle and aunt for a few years, saving her money, studied hard and eventually was admitted to

Eastern Washington State College. It took her six years because she had to work full time, but she eventually received her bachelor's degree and became a teacher. She was the first person in the history of her family to receive a college degree—and a woman, at that!

She taught for a few years, met and married my grandfather and became a wonderful mother to six children. She knew that you can do anything you desire if you believe strongly enough in your dream and were persistent and willing to work hard. She passed this on to her children and grandchildren who all consider Beatrice Grazziola to be their strongest role model.

Three Reasons Why You Should Continue Onward

This exercise should really be titled: *Why I should continue on my path of soul purpose expression when what I really want to do is give up.* We have all had these feelings. Life is too hard and you don't want to get out of bed. Yet, it is in the darkest moments that we must surrender. When we reach this point, a new life emerges. But until that time, we need reminders. For some of us, we want to continue because of our families, our children or our loved ones. For others, the drive to succeed won't allow us to give up. Perhaps we have family members whose lives were destroyed by alcoholism or drug abuse, and their destruction inspires us to continue.

Write down on another piece of paper the three reasons why you should continue on your path to true genius expression, especially when you don't think you can.

Foundation 2
"Three Reasons Why I Should Continue On When I'd Rather Give Up"
Example

Reason #1:

I could not look at myself in the mirror every day if I gave up on my dream to become a large-animal veterinarian. I have wanted to be one since I was a small child and I still want this more than anything, in spite of the fact that my parents are opposed and won't pay for my education. It's not a profession suitable for a woman (in other words, no self-respecting man would marry a woman who doctored cows).

Reason #2:

I've told my grandmother about my dream and she will be very disappointed in me if I don't follow my passion. Grandma said one of her biggest disappointments in life was not becoming a singer. It wasn't considered a proper activity for a young woman in her day, so she didn't do it.

Reason #3:

If Rebecca, my cousin, can become a doctor, I can be a veterinarian. I'm just as smart and capable as she is. Helping animals get well is just as important and worthy a profession as helping people get well.

Three People Who Really Believe in Me

It only takes one person to believe in you for you to continue. One of the most precious gifts that anyone can give another person is the expression of the statement, "I believe in you . . . " Over the years, I have been blessed with many friends, colleagues and family members who have encouraged me, nudged me, loved me enough to tell me the truth even when it sometimes hurt. My sister and brother-in-law have the top two lines on my people-who-really-believe-in-me list. Their support gave me the courage to finish ministerial school when I wanted to quit. Their encouragement caused me to continue my recovery work when it was most difficult. Comments like, "You can do it . . . ," "We love you enough to tell you that you are screwing up . . . ," "We really believe in you . . . go for it," give you extra energy to do what needs to be done. Support from another person refreshes our soul, heals our wounds, repairs our broken hearts. People don't acknowledge themselves or others enough, which is why when we receive it, it feels like a cool drink on a hot summer day.

A friend may well be reckoned the masterpiece of nature.

Ralph Waldo Emerson

Write down on a separate piece of paper the names and phone numbers of three people you can call on at any time for support.

Foundation 3
"People I Can Call On for Support"
Example

Suzy Smith   Phone #:   111-222-3333

John Q. Public   Phone #:   444-555-6666

Ezmiralda V. Pfanthauser   Phone #:   777-888-9999

Affirmations That Inspire Me

Affirmations are positive statements of your intention. Throughout the day, we all have inner conversations taking place, often without our conscious awareness. When the times get tough, our internal conversation may sound like this: "I can't go on. Life is just too hard. Maybe I wasn't supposed to follow my dream. Guess I'm just a failure . . . " Remember, your subconscious mind cannot differentiate between your internal conversations and reality. If your internal dialogue is negative, then your subconscious is supporting you in the beliefs that you cannot accomplish what you desire. Affirmations help us to stop the internal negative chatter and focus on positive thoughts. Positive affirmations must be concise and to the point, written in the present tense and have an emotional punch to them. On a fourth piece of paper write your affirmations. Be sure to personalize them with your name. Make sure they are statements that enflame your passions to achieve your goals, and are simple but catchy enough to be repeated 25 times a day. Here are a few examples of positive affirmations:

Foundation 4
"Positive Affirmations"
Example

1. I, Wanda, through the power of my divine creativity, inspire people around the world to make positive life changes.

2. I, Susan, am easily guided to find and own my beautiful, new home.

3. I, John, sail to exotic places around the world.

Spiritual Communities and Support Groups

When you participate in spiritual communities, such as Christian churches, synagogues, Buddhist or Hindu temples, New Thought centers, and others, you open yourself up to the possibility of extraordinary support from like-minded people. Similarly, joining a 12-step or recovery support group will provide the kind of loving support you need to make changes and grow spiritually. Make sure you surround yourself with people who believe in you even when you don't. If you don't already belong to such a group, shop around and try some out. Look for a group which is compatible with your spiritual belief system, and which can offer you love and encouragement.

Your completed Foundations include the people who inspire you, the names of people who believe in you and can buoy you up in down moments, reasons why you should continue even when things are tough, positive affirmations to guide your subconscious, and a spiritual support group. Keep these exercises handy and refer to them whenever you need encouragement. When you get down or discouraged, call the people on your list and ask for their help and support, and visit your spiritual support group. Your foundational support system is essential for maintaining your courage as you re-align yourself toward your soul purpose and accept more love into your life.

Statements of the Soul

The Statements of the Soul exercises assist you in stepping into your own personal authority by defining your own unique identity. The Statement of Truth reveals to you what you believe to be true about living a successful life. The Personal Vision Statement is to you what a keel is to a sailboat. It keeps you upright and moving forward as you sail through the waters of life. The Bio (short for biography) is a description of your accomplishments and the professional output of your creative energies. As you write these statements, do so from the perspective of your ideal future. In other words, write these statements about your greatest creative endeavors as though you have already accomplished them.

For example, one of my students wanted to be an actor, but her dream seemed ridiculous and outrageously impossible. She was having a very difficult time and came to class in tears. "It's just too big a dream," she cried. With some encouragement from her classmates, she did the Statements of the Soul just for fun and began to have a paradigm shift. Becoming an actor began to seem possible to her. By the end of class she had committed to us to enroll in an acting class at her local community college. She had leaned into her fear, done the exercises, and was able to move forward towards her dream.

Statement of Truth

Guidelines for writing your Statement of Truth are:

1.   The statement expresses what you stand for—what your values are.

2.   The statement is a summation of your keys to personal happiness and success. If you wanted to write a final statement defining your key to success to a loved one before departing this earth, what would be your words of wisdom.

3.   Keep the statement to 35 words or less. (This is a single statement, not a philosophical treatise.)

Statements of Truth:
Examples

❖   Each of us is responsible for the quality of our own life.

We become fully self-actualized and live our soul purpose *only* when we listen to and act upon the guidance of our inner wisdom.

❋   All the answers to any question we may have are within us.

❋   It took me a long time to realize that I am responsible for who I am today. When I took charge of me, my life changed and I found happiness.

Personal Vision Statements

A personal vision statement is much like a mission statement for a business. A business mission statement usually contains the reason for its existence (i.e., producing a product, providing a service), the way in which this will be accomplished (i.e., using contract employees, providing the service via the Internet), its intended market or audience (i.e., working women, people who buy stocks and bonds, children who watch Saturday morning TV), and sometimes qualifying statements as to the quality level of their offering. Likewise, a personal vision statement is your declaration of the reason for your existence; it is the heart of your soul purpose.

Guidelines for writing your Personal Vision Statement:

1.   The vision statement expresses your reason for existence. It should be positive.

2.   It states your impact on humanity.

3.   It should be 35 words or less.

4. It can change over time.

5. It can be used as a motivator when times get tough.

6. It can be memorized and used in a daily meditation.

Vision Statements:
Examples

❖ I, Jae Allen, exist to inspire through example and encouragement, the promotion of peace among all people, while fostering the actualization of each person's potential.

❖ Through the power of my inspired creativity, I, Jody Stevenson, share the images of my own transformation in order to ignite the genius in others, thereby creating a world of peace, prosperity, harmony and joy.

Bio

Your Bio (biographical sketch) should be a short paragraph about you and your accomplishments written as if it appeared on the back jacket of your most recent book, or in a newspaper article about your most recent achievements. It is set in a time when you have already accomplished your dreams, but no date should be mentioned. This gives you permission to do what you want to do. The Bio should be more than just a statement of facts, it should summarize what most delights you about the expression of your soul purpose.

Bio
Examples

❋ Jody M. Stevenson, author and professional speaker, draws from 20 years of experience teaching thousands of people nationally how to ignite their inner genius and create a life of success based on soul purpose principles. Her specialty is assisting others to clarify and then manifest their personal vision, while mastering the transition process. She delights in coaching people as they awaken to their potential and personal passions. Jody is in private practice as a counselor. She is presently working on her next book.

❋ Rosa Elise Rubin, noted writer, artist and nature spokesperson, received recognition today from the North American president for her work tuning people into their connectedness to the natural world. For years, she has been giving lectures and conducting workshops on this theme as well as how we influence and impact nature. She shows through experiential activities that all things in nature have spirit and are ruled by the spirit realm. Once people are able to communicate with nature, she guides them to express their feelings in physical form through writing, drawing or other creative outlets. Rosa has also acted as spokesperson for nature's interests at various decision-making events around the world, and has written several books about our links to nature.

Congratulate yourself. You have just completed a large body of work in defining who you really are. You have seriously begun the process of rediscovering your soul purpose.

Being of Service

There was an eight-year-old girl in San Francisco who had a life-threatening illness. She desperately needed a blood transfusion but she had an unusual blood type. After looking nationwide for a suitable blood donor, the doctors discovered that her six-year-old brother shared her rare blood type. The little boy's mother and the doctor approached him and asked if he would be willing to donate his blood to save his sister. He wanted to think about it so they agreed to wait a day for his answer. The next day, he agreed to donate his blood and the process was begun. As the brother shared his life-giving blood with his sister, it was immediately apparent that this transfusion was working as healthy color began to return to the little girl's body. The brother, however, was becoming more and more agitated. Finally, he called over the doctor and asked him in a quiet, small voice, "Doctor, am I going to die soon or will it take awhile?" You see, the little boy had thought he had to give all his blood to his sister!

This true story describes the ultimate gift of giving—a willingness to give up one's life for the sake of another. Being in service, however, is not life-threatening but life-enhancing. To give away and share your divinely-given talents with the rest of humanity is the ultimate thank-you for the gift of those talents. Through our willingness to share our special gifts, we can experience an important payback—the joy of being creative. Secondary paybacks may include increased abundance in the form of money, opportunities and recognition. Ultimately, the greatest payback from sharing your gifts with others is the deep, internal knowing that you are contributing to the uplifting of the consciousness of humanity.

As you step into your willingness to share your greatness with others, do so with enthusiasm and authority, for your sharing is a statement of what is important to you. Become excited about who you are and what you do best. Most of us in childhood learn to be apologetic for who we are—to belittle our abilities. But this is false modesty. You are not being grateful for the wonderful gifts which have blessed you. Instead, be pleased and proud of who you uniquely are. I find it fascinating that the volunteers in our organization who give of their time and talents with self-appreciation and authority are the first to be offered jobs. If you are jobless right now and are seeking a place to develop your soul purpose, volunteer for organizations that service your special interests.

My friend Jae has a very special gift of working with people who are making their transition. He brings his sense of peace and contentment, along with his deep understanding of the eternal processes of life, to the sharing of his talents in a uniquely compassionate way. He creates an atmosphere of sacred energy and love for both the dying person and the family members. He is fully aware that the Great Creator is his source, and as he generously gives his time and talents and invoices the Universe (see Chapter 6), he is richly rewarded. He lives in a beautiful home, wears wonderful clothes, travels often and has numerous opportunities to experience abundance. He is a perfect example of someone who has stepped into his soul purpose with authority and enthusiasm, and is willing to serve humanity.

When I first moved to Seattle, I was told, "In the Northwest, you have mountains, ocean, desert and plains. If, by chance, Jody, you are bored, it is indeed your own fault." This simple admonition resonated with my heart and taught me a valuable life lesson. There are always people to serve, talents and skills to nurture, causes to support, creativity to express, and most important, your soul purpose to pursue. If you are bored, I respectfully and lovingly say, "It is your own fault." Be willing to open up your mind and heart so that you can attract opportunities that support you. Decide what really excites you. Find an organization that supports your interests. Make that call today. Give one hour a week with enthusiasm and authority, and do something that you love to do. When doing this, you become the hands, feet and heart of the Great Creator. Your willingness to share yourself will open you up to many unexpected opportunities. Being in service to others will reveal and nurture your soul purpose.

Declaration of Soul Purpose Action

The Declaration of Soul Purpose Action is an exercise that gives you an opportunity to state how you have been sabotaging your own creative genius and how you want to change this. Spend some time analyzing your behavior and thought patterns, and write down three ways you are limiting your ability to succeed in your dreams. Then write down three ways you can alter your behavior and thought patterns to enhance your successes.(See example on page 109.) Commit to do those things for 21 days. After three weeks of conscientious effort, you should be well on your way to permanently improving the quality of your life and realizing your soul purpose.

Declaration of Soul Purpose Action

I, _____ , am an expression of the Divine. I know that I have a choice in how I express my creativity every day. I realize that as I consciously express my talents and skills, and open myself up the fulfillment of my dreams, my life unfolds harmoniously and prosperously.

I understand that how and when I express my creativity is the key to my success. As I review my life, I recognize there are ways I sabotage success in my everyday life. Therefore, for the next 21 days, I release the following success-stopping actions:

1. I no longer belittle my talents and skills to myself or to others.
2. I no longer work at jobs that I hate or that violate my personal values.
3. I no longer dwell on the negative things in my life and in the world around me.

I joyfully commit to do the following success-enhancing activities:

1. I practice daily imagining my desired future using all my senses.
2. I now create a volunteer opportunity in an area that interests me.
3. I honor my body by eating healthy meals, exercising regularly, getting sufficient sleep and meditating daily.

_____
Signature

_____
Date

6

CREATIVE EXPRESSION

Divine Creativity

❊ ***Creativity*** is the expression of your divine energies.

❊ ***Genius creativity*** is the conscious awareness and expression of your creative powers and divine energies.

> *Man is asked to make of himself what he is supposed to become to fulfill his destiny.*
>
> **Paul Tillich**

When I ask my students how they express themselves creatively, I get the usual answers: "I paint, I sing, I dance, I write novels, I act, I do gourmet cooking, I yodel . . ." And of course, many students say simply, and with true belief, "I am not creative." Well, our normal definition of creativity is too narrow. Since we co-create our lives through our thoughts, then every human being is enormously creative and is creating every moment he or she is alive. Every aspect of our lives is a form of creative expression: our health, our relationships, our prosperity, our recreation and our work. But most people remain totally unaware of their co-creative power.

When we create our lives, consciously or unconsciously, we are tapping into the natural energy flow of the Universe. To tap into our creative energies and use them consciously is to live life spiritually. To live life spiritually is to have a relationship with something greater than ourselves, which is the source of all life, the Great Creator. If we open ourselves consciously to the universal creative force, we become a channel for the Great Creator to express through us. Genius creativity is the conscious awareness and expression of our creative powers and our divine energies. A powerful way to begin the day is to give thanks upon awakening to the Great Creator for our ability to express and experience life, and then to offer our talents and abilities to humanity in the ways that the Great Creator would use them.

I myself do nothing. The Holy Spirit accomplishes all through me.

William Blake

Creativity in the Workplace

Most American adults below retirement age spend the biggest chunks of their time sleeping or working. What we do for our job—and that includes being a parent and homemaker—is the primary focus of our adult years. But, a very large percentage of Americans are unhappy in the workplace (according to many research findings, percentages range as high as 85-97%), and the most heart attacks occur between 7:00 and 9:00 AM on Mondays, the beginning of the work week for most people. Many hate what they are doing because it is boring, stressful or physically difficult; or they hate the boss, their co-workers, or the work environment; or they feel unappreciated, exploited or under-valued. While a large percentage of people are unhappy with how they spend their days, they feel trapped by the need for a regular income and benefits.

Another group of discontented workers has arisen in recent

years due to corporate down-sizing and the need to increase productivity. These are often professionals who like what they do but find the long hours, intense stress and lack of personal time physically, mentally, emotionally and spiritually exhausting. High salaries and fear of the pink slip keep these people tied to these corporate sweat shops.

Jobs in most western cultures have become not only the source of income, but the source of our identity as well. But for many of us, our work identity is at odds with who we really are. A job should be an expression of your natural energy flow—an expression of your soul purpose. When you are living your soul purpose, you create a way to earn a living based on your desires, goals, skills and talents. When this happens, your creativity will flow unimpeded, and you will look forward to doing your work. Your job will be an expression of your own unique genius, rather than an often ill-fitting cloak of identity you put on for 8–12 hours a day.

Characteristics of Creative Expression in the Workplace

How can you tell whether your source of employment is just a job, or is an expression of your soul purpose? First of all, how you feel about getting up each day to do your work is a very good indicator. If you dread Monday mornings, or whenever your work week begins, then you most likely have a job. If you look forward to doing your work, you may be expressing your soul purpose. But there are other factors that determine whether your work is an expression of your soul purpose. And because of the multiple factors, there are many stages of work expression between Job and Soul Purpose Work. To help you determine how to evaluate your work expression, I have created three categories: Job, Career and Soul Purpose Work.

❖   A *job* is an activity you do to earn money.

❖   A *career* is work for which you have been trained but which may or may not be fulfilling.

✣   *Soul purpose work* is the expression of one's spiritual essence and one's destiny; it is fulfilling, fun and financially rewarding.

✣   *Skills* are things you have learned to do, but which may or may not be things you like to do.

✣   *Talents* are things you are innately good at doing, and which make you happy when you are doing them.

The chart on pages 116-118 shows the characteristics of creative expression in these three situations in the workplace. The traits are attributes about each basic situation which will help you determine whether you have a job, a career or are expressing your soul purpose. The chart is based on research I've conducted with my clients and students.

It is likely that your answers may fall into more than one category. If so, use your own judgment to determine which category applies to you, and use the traits to show you where things need to change. Put emphasis, however, first on determining your soul purpose, and then on finding or creating the work which allows you to express your genius creativity.

The Soul Purpose Definition of Success

All people delight in the idea of success. You and I, by virtue of being human, have a deep desire to be successful, happy and self-actualized. We yearn to have peaceful days, harmonious relationships, perfect health and financial freedom. We have an inner urge to seek outlets for our divinely-given creative talents and to be richly rewarded for expressing these. We want to do our share in uplifting the consciousness of humanity and to leave this world a better place because of our contribution.

This desire for success is the divine urging of our soul purpose to be expressed. All forms of nature experience this. The rose seed desires to grow into a beautiful flowering rose bush. The acorn stretches upward to become a majestic oak tree. A newborn baby wants to create a magnificent life and it comes into the world with all the wisdom, intelligence and power needed to do that. We can deny this urge to be magnificent; we can ignore it or push it away, but it quietly waits for us to discover the Universal Laws of Life and then to consciously obey its principles. Fortunately for us, this divine urge to be happy will not leave us alone.

What is Success?

To laugh often and love much;
To win the respect of intelligent persons and the affection
      of children;
To earn the approval of honest critics and endure the betrayal
      of false friends;

To appreciate beauty;
To give of yourself without the slightest thought of return;
To have accomplished a task.
To have played and laughed with enthusiasm and sung with
      exaltation;
To know that even one life has breathed easier because you
      have lived;
This is to have succeeded.

                                        Anonymous

Success, by definition, means "a favorable termination of a venture." It is a concept that defines the result when the unlimited potential of the Universe is channeled into individual expression. When you are expressing your creative energies and doing what you love to do, then you are living a life of success. And you are successful because you have allowed yourself to

Characteristics of Creative Expression in the Workplace

Attitude about your job: This is the test of how much you look forward to your work each day.

Job	Have to work
Career	Want to work
Soul Purpose Work	Passionate about your work

Who controls and availability of opportunities for growth and development: Do you control your opportunities for job and skill expansion, or do others, such as your boss or the union?

Job	Limited opportunities; others control
Career	Moderate opportunities; mix of you and others control
Soul Purpose Work	Unlimited opportunities because you create them; you control

Place on the Skill-Talent continuum: How much of what you do is utilizing your talents—those things you innately love to do and have a special aibility to do—and how much uses your skills—what you have been trained to do?

Job	Use of skills
Career	Use of skills and some talents
Soul Purpose Work	Use of talents and skills, but talents dominate

Risk of negative wear and tear on the body, mind and soul: Does your work renew you because you enjoy it, or is it debilitating for your body, mind or spirit?

Job	High risk because it is unsatisfying
Career	Medium risk because it is a mix of satisfying and unsatisfying
Soul Purpose Work	Low risk because it is very satisfying

Willingness to live one's bigger dream: Does your job support your soul purpose dreams or is it just a way to earn a living that stifles your dreams?

Job	None to low willingness; your dreams are stifled
Career	Moderate willingness; some aspects of your dreams are realized
Soul Purpose Work	High willingness because you are living your dreams

Public acceptance of your work expression: How do others respond to the way you express your creativity through work?

Job	No public criticism because you are doing what others want or expect you to do
Career	No or some public criticism depending how much your dream is in conflict with other people's expectations
Soul Purpose Work	Often high public criticism, at least initially, if your soul purpose is in conflict with other people's expectations or values

Motivation for work: Why do you work; what besides money do you get from your work?

Job	Security; works for money to pay bills
Career	Mix of security and destiny; works to pay bills and for self-expression
Soul Purpose Work	Destiny; works for self-expression; knows financial self-sufficiency will be a natural outcome of self-expression

Source of direction in work (daily activities and job choices): Are you able to determine when, how and why you work, or do others do this?

Job	Other-directed
Career	Other- and self-directed
Soul Purpose Work	Self-directed

Impact on one's creative expression: Is your work an expression of who you really are and does it support and further your soul purpose?

Job	Stifling
Career	Acknowledging
Soul Purpose Work	Expanding

accept the riches of life as you define them.

Success must be defined solely by the individual person and not by the culture, the society, or the expectations of your family or friends. The context of success will be the society or culture, but your personal definition of success must be based on your soul purpose in order to be truly your own. Because of this, one person's definition of success will be different from another's. My definition of success may seem outrageous and impossible to some, while others may say I am being much too limited. In truth, there is no right or wrong. Success is an individual experience.

We experience life in four basic areas: health, relationships, prosperity and creative expression. If we are struggling in any of these four areas, we are not experiencing a happy life. Each area is intertwined with the others. While it may be the norm to struggle in one or more areas, it is natural to be peaceful, joyful, harmonious, prosperous and healthy in every aspect of our lives. We need only to define our ideal life—what success means to us in each of these four areas, then believe in ourselves, and create it.

Success, then, is the expression of our soul's desire. In other words, to experience success, we must become so familiar with our talents, skills, strengths, dreams and our basic philosophy that even in the face of a perceived failure, we can keep marching on. We forge ahead into uncharted territory and never let go of our desires or our willingness to grow. The dreams we have are the whisperings of our soul . . . nudging us to stay focused and believe in ourselves. If we lose focus or falter in our self-belief, we are choosing to honor our limitations instead. Living a limited life can be more comfortable for some, but as our soul purpose is unveiled and we experience more success in our lives, we are led away from our comfort zone and closer to the manifestation of our dreams.

Successful Failure

I used to have a Comfort Zone
where I knew I couldn't fail.
The same four walls of busy work,
were really more like a jail.

I longed so much to do the things
I'd never done before.
But I stayed inside my Comfort Zone,
and paced the same old floor.

I claimed to be so busy,
with the things inside my zone.
But deep inside I longed for
something special of my own.

I couldn't let my life go by,
just watching others win.
I held my breath and stepped outside
to let the change begin.

I took a step and with new strength
I'd never felt before,
I kissed my Comfort Zone "good-bye"
and closed and locked the door.

If you are in a Comfort Zone,
afraid to venture out,
Remember that all winners were
at one time filled with doubt.

A step or two and words of praise,
can make your dreams come true.
Greet your future with a smile,
Success is there for you!

Anonymous

Ironically, human beings are the only species that has the ability to thwart its own destiny. The rose does not apologize for its beauty. The oak tree does not secretly yearn to be a dwarf Bamboo. A newborn baby does not come into this world hoping to lead a life of pain, sorrow, lack and limitation. His or her natural, innate desire is to be free, happy and successful.

But humans are conditioned to expect less than our potential. At a very young age, we begin to hear thoughts and ideas about how limited we are. We are told we can't, shouldn't, and ought not to do certain things, to think certain thoughts, or to pursue our dreams. The more we hear and believe these limiting thoughts, the more we shrink our expectations and see ourselves as limited. We then begin to experience an imbalance in life. Our health deteriorates, or our relationships are inharmonious and dysfunctional; we are lacking in prosperity or our jobs become painful and unrewarding. In the chaos and turmoil of the everyday struggle, we forget our divine perfection. We cease to listen to our inner voice that has the ability to guide and direct us to levels of success far beyond our wildest dreams.

Research has shown that by the age of 65, 55 out of 100 people will need financial, emotional or physical help. More than 50% of humanity has accepted beliefs about themselves that have caused them to live limited, struggling lives. Another 42 people will be more independent, prosperous and healthy, but will still need some help from others. Only 3 out of every 100 people will be self-actualized. They will have achieved, and will continue to achieve, their true potential—their soul purpose. A good example of this is Jacque-Yves Cousteau, the well-known ocean explorer, environmentalist, inventor and activist for future generations. Now in his mid-eighties, he continues to actively participate in his dream and to pass on his vision to others. He understands at a most fundamental level the connectedness of all creatures to the earth, and the precariousness of life on this planet. Compare this self-actualized being to the average elderly inhabitant of a nursing home!

Self-actualized individuals remember the greatest of all universal principles: that there is a unifying connection between the Great Creator and humans, between all humans, and between humans and all other inhabitants of this earth. They recognize there is an unlimited source of energy out of which all is created. They are so steeped in divine energy that their lives exude unlimited energy. They have lifted themselves out of mediocrity and into a manifested life of mastery. In other words, they have listened to the genius of their soul, and have discovered the real purpose for their existence. They have ignored their limited human programming and stepped into their soul purpose.

The Role of Belief

If you think you are beaten, you are;
If you think you dare not, you don't;
If you'd like to win, but you think you can't,
It's almost a cinch you won't;
If you think you'll lose, you've lost,
For out in the world you'll find
Success begins with a fellow's will;
It's all in the state of mind.

Anonymous

At the University of Chicago, 100 students were studied who were extraordinarily successful in the areas of academics, music or athletics. It was found that the common denominator of success for these students was not their IQ or their training, the common denominator was a strong belief in themselves. In fact, many others had more training or higher IQ's, but for these 100 students, they *believed* that they could achieve, and they achieved to the extent of their belief.

As we step into the light of our soul purpose, we boldly say, *"This* is who I am; *this* is my chosen life style and *this* is how I choose to express my greatness!" Sometimes, people with whom we have shared our lives feel threatened as we begin to express at a higher level. As we move closer to our genius, we change and when we change, we are asking, usually subconsciously, other people in our lives to change also. Some will be there to support and cheer us on; some people will watch us from the sidelines, waiting for us to fail; some will be highly critical and leave the relationship. When this happens, you may feel grief-stricken, confused and sad. These feelings are appropriate to the process of letting go. It may seem easier to turn back and return to the old you, but once you have decided to experience your genius, Life supports you in staying focused and in moving forward.

The Meaning of Failure

Human beings have an intense fear of failure. "God forbid," I hear my students say, "that I might begin to fulfill my dreams, go for the vision burning within me, step out into my authentic genius self . . . and fail!" When I ask them for a definition of failure, I receive answers like, "I might look stupid," or "So-and-so may not like it," or "What will people say?"

My response to these fears is: "You are right!! You may look stupid to some, especially when you are starting out. Some people may not like what you are doing, and many people will talk about you. Expect it! Make it okay! Even if you are criticized, condemned, laughed at and not supported, choose to believe in yourself, for your actions are bringing you closer to realizing your soul purpose!"

Failure may be a signal that the path we are currently on is not, or is no longer, a viable path for us. Or failure may be a signal that something in our lives—some thought pattern or behavior—is no longer working for our highest good. As you scan your life for failures, you have the opportunity to forgive yourself. In every failure there is a cosmic gift of awareness. The experience of failure can be a teacher when we purposefully look for love in all our endeavors. What we labeled failure in the past has often been the impetus to move us to the next level of our greatness. Failure is always an opportunity to get to know our-selves at a deeper level. The journey to self-discovery is love in action, especially in times of failure.

Soul-purposed people are willing to fail in the human sense because they recognize that spiritually there is no such thing as failure. Failure is only a judgment of a result. *What we call a fail-ure is only a result that did not turn out the way we wanted or ex-pected it to.* Life experiences only become failures when we de-fine them that way. The essence of any result is only energy. The judgment is attached to that energy by social expectations and rules.

Peak performers are motivated by pleasing results. Failure-prone people are motivated by pleasing methods.

***Success* magazine.**

Examples of Successful Failures

Soul-purposed people are willing to make mistakes, look fool-ish and fail in the eyes of others. They are willing to be judged, criticized and even ostracized. They realize that in any creative endeavor, chaos and upset are natural by-products of the pro-cess. They accept and give thanks for failure in their lives, realiz-ing that failure is only feedback on what does or doesn't bring them closer to their goal. Thomas Edison, the great inventor, was once asked by a friend, "Are you going to have ten thousand failures?" (There was a rumor that Edison had failed 9,999 times while he tried to find the answer to producing the incandescent light.)

"Ten-thousand failures?" Edison replied, "I didn't fail. I just discovered 9,999 ways not to invent the electric light bulb." He knew he had not failed but was gathering information.

In industrial cultures, success is usually determined by the amount of goods we possess and our status—either professional or social. A new client walked into my office one day. Jerry was in every sense a corporate success. His title offered him status and clout; his salary gave him money for a luxurious life; he traveled all over the world on a generous expense account; his fancy car impressed people. By everyday standards, he was extremely successful. But he was not happy. As he talked during our first meeting, he said, "I have it all: status, money, things. I am materially filled up and spiritually bankrupt. I am exhausted, fried and frazzled. I have it all and I am a failure."

Over the next few weeks, as he began to uncover and define what his spiritual values were, his genius self began to emerge. He learned to view his old life with compassion and understanding. As he began to rediscover his soul purpose, he changed his priorities—putting his soul qualities first and his material accomplishments second. With the intensity and focus that had obviously carried him to the top of the corporate world, he dove into the truth of who he really was. Emerging out of this corporate denizen was a new man—softer, kinder and more gentle. After a few weeks of processing what he called his failure, he began to realize that this divine discontent was a spiritual wake-up call. The need of his soul purpose to express itself had become so strong that he could no longer deny it.

Jerry had developed many worthwhile skills during his corporate years and he had many to place on his Developed Skills Sacred Circle. Over time he came to recognize his many innate talents, who his ideal audience was and what dreams had yet to be manifested. Most important, because he was so willing to move through the process, he discovered his true self. The voice of his true self—his quiet, still voice—became his daily top priority. "Any task can and will wait for me to go inward and listen," he would say with a twinkle in his eye. Over several months, Jerry changed his life dramatically and brought it into alignment with his soul purpose.

In prosperous times, you put it in your pocket. In the down times, you put it in your heart.

Les Brown

Another young man was a constant failure. At the age of 21, his business failed. He was defeated in a legislative race at the age of 22. Another business failed at age 24. He was devastated by the death of his sweetheart when he was 26. He had a nervous breakdown when he was 27. At the age of 34, he lost a congressional race. He lost another congressional race at the age of 36. He lost a senatorial race at the age of 45. He failed in his efforts to become vice president at the age of 47. He lost another senatorial race at the age of 49. But, at the age of 52, Abraham Lincoln succeeded in becoming the 16th president of the United States and made a lasting impact on the course of our country.

Many people would have given up all hope of a political career after the first defeat, but Abraham Lincoln experienced many situations that the public called failures and he did not let them keep him from trying again and again. Belief in failure is a way of poisoning the mind. Fear of failure cripples and atrophies our willingness to try. What we call failure is *always* a spiritual wake-up call. How we choose to perceive a situation is *always* up to us. Failure exists only in the mind. It happens to teach us something—not to stop us from accomplishing what we must.

Success Exercise

The following exercise is intended to help you identify the good that has come out of any failure in your life. What message did the failure have for you? Did it re-direct your life? Did a new, more compatible person come into your life after the end of a relationship? Did you learn self-reliance or did you gain personal strength when someone or something didn't turn out the way you expected?

A friend of mine was laid off from his job when his company closed. He had worked for this and the parent company for over 20 years and he had a great deal of experience, skill and training. He assumed that he would be hired by another company within a matter of a few weeks. Well, every door he knocked on remained closed. He fell into a severe depression and lost his self-confidence. Then a friend connected him to an organization that helped people learn how to job-hunt effectively. This man learned how to appreciate his skills and talents, he learned how to network and how to interview and negotiate a salary. He eventually

CREATIVE EXPRESSION ❖ 127

found a good job with good compensation. The process took him nine months. Finding a good job was rewarding, but the true reward for him was a tremendous sense of personal growth. He recognized what he truly loved to do. Then he learned how to effectively sell himself and how to use the job-hunting system to his advantage. The gift of his initial failure at finding a job opened to him many opportunities for personal discovery.

The Success Exercise begins with an opportunity to list three successes in your life. This is to provide balance—I don't want you to focus solely on those times when things didn't turn out to your advantage. Then it moves you on to list three significant failures; choose events or situations that seemed like the end of the world when they happened. Analyze each one for the gift that came from that event. This gift may not have happened immediately, so if one isn't apparent, go out further into your future and see how this event or situation changed your life. You may need to ask family or close friends to help you see how this failure changed you. Once you are aware of the gift, record this and show how it affected the course of your life.

What would you do if you knew you could not fail? What would you give yourself permission to explore if you were guaranteed success as you define it? Living life at the edge of our current reality frees us to expand, explore and to seize the possibilities available to us. It frees us to step into our soul purpose and experience our genius self.

People are always blaming their circumstances for what they are. I don't believe in circumstances. The people who get on in this world are the people who get up and look for the circumstances they want, and if they can't find them, make them!

George Bernard Shaw

Examples of Success
Exercise

The top three successes, or accomplishments in my life are:

1. Going to college and obtaining a degree.
2. Learning to scuba dive when I'm claustrophobic.

3.   Reaching a deep level of peace with my parents.

The top three failures I have experienced in my life are:

1.   Many dysfunctional relationships.
2.   Claiming bankruptcy.
3.   Undertaking numerous diets but continuing to gain weight.

From the first failure, the success that came out of it was: It led me into a 12-step program.

From the second failure, the success that came out of it was: I began to educate myself about the spiritual laws of abundance.

From the third failure, the success that came out of it was: I learned more about health and well-being.

I am grateful for my first failure because: I developed inner strength and learned to love myself.

I am grateful for my second failure because: I learned how to value my gifts and be richly rewarded for them.

I am grateful for my third failure because: I am learning how to honor my sacred physical temple.

Putting Soul in Your Goals

Goals are the end-points towards which efforts are directed. When properly constructed, goals are concrete and specific. They provide us a focus for our creative energies. Without such a focus, our energies become scattered and weakened. A lack of focus can bring on a feeling of being frayed at the edges or burned out. Without goals, without focus, our chance of being successful is limited.

We must become like water flowing down a mountain. When water has a direction and can follow the law of gravity to the ocean, it has the ability to carve out a path from the solid stone of the mountainside to achieve its goal. As the water creates a creek or riverbed, this keeps the water contained and speeds up its journey toward its goal. When water is unable to follow the flow of gravity, or create a channel to contain its flow, it slows down, spreads out into a swamp or lake, and sometimes stagnates or dries up.

This is also true for human beings. The Universal Law of Genius is our gravity; it pulls us to step into our greatness—our soul purpose. Without focus, we can spread our energies too thin, stagnate or dry up. By focusing our energies, we have the ability to carve out a river bank in the energy field of unlimited possibilities—our mountainside. Goal-setting is the way we focus our energies.

To be useful channels for the flow of our soul energies, goals must be concrete and measurable. If your goal is "I want to be a good person," that is neither concrete nor measurable. How do you know when you've become a "good person." How *good* is good? Do you have to be as selfless and giving as Mother Theresa, or is it your desire just to improve on some areas of your life. If by "good person" you really mean you want to be more generous and kind, you might create a goal that said, "I will give 5% of my income for this year to charity," or "I will give positive feedback to a friend, colleague or stranger at least once every day." Both of these goals are very specific and measurable. You know if they are achievable and realistic, and you know if they move you towards your soul purpose.

Unless your goal is beyond that which you have mastered . . . you will not grow.

Osborne

As you write down your goals, it is essential to ask yourself if these are truly *your* goals. You need to insure that your goals reflect the desires of your soul purpose and are not the reflection of your parents', spouse's, teachers' or friends' desires, or society's expectations. Ask yourself about each goal, does this goal bring me closer to my soul purpose? If it doesn't, then decide whether it is something you want to spend time and energy focusing on.

Write down your goals and read them daily. By constantly reminding yourself of your goals, you will begin to adjust your life so that it moves in alignment with your soul purpose, and you will begin to live from a position of personal power. As you read your goals daily, begin to embody them in your life.

My Soul Purpose Goals
Example

Goal 1:   I will sign up for a community college class to study physical therapy. This goal advances my soul purpose in the following way: I will begin to learn the new skills necessary to become a physical therapist.

Goal 2:   I will volunteer at the local hospital. This goal advances my soul purpose in the following way: I will gain the experience of hands-on learning and the richness of helping others.

Goal 3:   I will find a job in a biological laboratory. This goal advances my soul purpose in the following way: I will develop professional relationships and enhance my ability to network.

Invoicing the Universe

Compensation is unlimited for the rightful use of our creative energies and divinely-given talents. To be richly rewarded for the expression of our unique abilities is to have high self-esteem. High self-esteem and prosperity are synonymous. There is no virtue in living a life of poverty or a martyred existence. Stuart Wilde, author of *Life was Never Meant to be a Struggle*, wrote, "Poverty is restriction, and, as such, it is the greatest injustice you can perpetuate upon yourself."

Physically, money is paper with ink on it. Spiritually, money is energy and thought. Money, in and of itself, has no value. What counts are the ideas and value we place on money. All opinions and judgments about money are nonsense because they are illusions. Change the ideas you have about money and you will change your experience of prosperity, no matter how much or how little you can currently call your own.

There are some basic rules for expanding your abundance:

❖ **Believe that you live in an abundant energy field.**

The best teacher about prosperity is nature. Go to a nearby tree and count the leaves or needles. Go to a beach, scoop up a handful of sand and try to count each grain. Next time it is snowing, try counting the falling snowflakes. This same abundance applies to us. We live in an abundant universe and our divine heritage is prosperity.

❖ **Realize that you deserve to have an abundant life and to be richly rewarded for using your creative energies.**

We are each unique expressions of the Great Creator with our own set of talents, skills and ideal audience. To express our soul purpose is the Great Creator's gift to us. When we express our soul purpose and share our gifts with others, we are acknowledging and returning this gift to the Great Creator. It is the desire of the Great Creator to richly reward us for the joyful expression of our talents.

❖   **Explore the concept that your only real boss is the Great Creator, even if you have a human boss.**

When we are living our soul purpose, the source of our instruction is the quiet voice of wisdom within us. This is the voice of the Great Creator—our ultimate boss. Our "job" is to follow its guidance and express our soul purpose. When we do this, we are truly *self-employed.* This does not preclude us from working for another human, but only suggests that the highest authority in our lives must be the expression of our soul purpose. It can, however, be expressed through the medium of another person's employ.

❖   **Learn to manage your money both spiritually and fiscally.**

In other words, learn about the spiritual laws of the Universe and develop good spending and savings habits. The spiritual laws of the Universe include the belief that we live in an abundant Universe, we are conduits for abundance, and we must circulate (give away) a portion of our abundance in order to keep receiving it. This means that we must learn to *receive* before we can *give* (we cannot give away something before we have first received it), and we need to keep the flow moving by giving away a portion of what we've received.

Here's how this works in real life terms: when you receive $1—or any amount of money, give away the first 10% to your spiritual source or another worthy cause; put the second 10% in savings and live off the remaining 80%. This is managing your money both spiritually and fiscally, and according to spiritual laws.

❖ **Be willing to "invoice the Universe" for every activity you do which uses your talents and skills in the furtherance of your soul purpose.**

Invoicing the Universe causes you to open your heart and your mind to new possibilities. It also causes you to recognize and acknowledge those things you are doing in support of your soul purpose goals. It expands your consciousness and liberates your thinking. For any and all outputs of your creative talents where you volunteer your services or where you are not paid full compensation, you will record this on an "Invoicing the Universe" sheet.

In order to charge the Universe, you first need to determine a monetary value for your time. This can be based on your current skill and talent level, provided they are applicable to your soul purpose, or you can base your rate on the hourly compensation you expect to receive when you are actively living your soul purpose. Or you can find some figure in between the two. The important point is to determine what you would charge recipients of your services if they were paying you. An example of this is a client I had who was actively working his "Invoice to the Universe." He is an accountant and he determined that his skills and talents are worth $53 an hour. When he spent an hour advising a new business on accounting matters, and they were only able to pay him $20, he charged the Universe for the remaining $33. When he volunteered his time, he charged the full $53 per hour.

Creating an Invoice to the Universe

Across the top of a sheet of paper, starting on the left side, write "Date." Moving towards the center, write "Activity," then "$ Amount." Then write "Payback," and then "Date Paid."

Date	Activity	$ Amount	Payback	Date Paid

To use your invoice, let's say you have realized that your soul purpose is to work with youth at risk—troubled kids, and your hourly rate is $50.00/hour. So you begin to volunteer for an organization that has many different events helping teenagers. For every hour you give of your time and talents, you charge your universal boss $50.00. Let's say you worked 8 hours one Saturday. 8 x $50.00 = $400.00.

Date	3/9/95
Activity	Worked at Teen Center
$ Amount	$400.00
Payback	
Date Paid	

Now you start to pay close attention to the details of your life. Anything that can be categorized as unexpected income—whether in actual dollars or in other benefits, such as a friend taking you to lunch, getting a free ride to San Francisco or getting a refund from the electric company—becomes your payback. See the invoice sample on the next page.

Date	3/9/95
Activity	Worked at Teen Center
$ Amount	$400.00
Payback	Ted bought me lunch, $15.00
Date Paid	4/10/95

No amount is too small or too big to put in this column. Again, what you focus on expands. When you begin to notice the positive things happening in your life, you will attract more positive things into your life. Your abundance expands as your consciousness expands.

	Invoice to the Universe *Example*			
Date	Activity	$ Amt	Payback	Date Paid
3/9/95	Worked at Teen Center: 8 hours	$400.00	Ted bought lunch: $15.00 free massage: $40.00 found $10.00 on street	4/10/95 4/24/95 4/27/95
3/17/95	Counseled teen at Center: 1 hour	$50.00	Mom bought me a sweater: $49.95	5/4/95
4/13/95	Helped conduct drug-free meeting at church: 2 hours	$100.00		

MOVING FORWARD

Reasons

His mother was in the kitchen preparing breakfast. "Time to get up, Honey, and get ready for school," she called to her son upstairs. A few minutes later, after hearing only silence, she yelled, "Son, get up; you will be late for school."

Silence again, with the clock still ticking. With irritation, she ran upstairs, flung open her son's bedroom door and found him still tucked in bed.

"Get up right now," the frazzled mother said, "Right NOW!"

"Why should I get up. I don't want to go to school!" her son shouted. "The teachers hate me and the kids make fun of me! Just give me two good reasons why I should go."

"Because, my dear son, you are 40 years old and you are the principal," she responded with exasperation.

We all have good excuses why we can't be soulful and purposeful in our lives. "I'm too busy," we say with authority. "Sure, I would like to, but I'm not educated . . . " "My kids, you know . . . no time for myself . . . don't have the money . . . " "My health, failing health . . . can't do it." "Sure wish I could, but my husband, well . . . he won't let me." "My wife, oh, she would get real upset if I started a new focus in my life . . . ." And the list goes on and on. When we believe in them, excuses become reasons.

Fortunately for us though, the Great Creator will not let us get off that easily. All that holds us back are false beliefs. We will, at some point on our path of eternity, say yes to our passions, liberate ourselves from bondage and boldly step into our soul purpose. No excuse, reason or person will be able to stop us!

When you are through changing, you are through.

Anonymous

We Are Like Penguins

As we learn about our great purpose, we humans are like baby penguins. They are not born knowing how to swim, but must learn in order to survive. When the time comes for the babies to leave the nest, the parent penguins jump off the ice flows into the icy waters of the Antarctic. The babies remain on the ice flow looking down at their parents who call to them to follow.

There are three distinct baby penguin attitudes toward this venture into the unknown. (Perhaps you can relate to one of them.) The first group of babies are very brave. When they see their parents swimming in the water and calling to them, they run to the edge of the flow and without hesitation leap into the water.

The second group hears their parents calling them, and they panic. Pacing back and forth, back and forth, these baby penguins worry and fret and call out with great concern. Their parents continue to beckon them to jump, encouraging them to take the next step in life. After a long arduous process of worry and fear, they leap, only to find they have the inner knowledge of how to swim.

The third group of penguin babies is just not ready to jump. No amount of family encouragement or positive role modeling by other babies can persuade this group to take the leap. Fear of the unknown paralyzes them and with stubborn determination, they refuse to move off their spot on the ice flow. (Does this sound familiar?) However, nature mercifully takes care of them because eventually the tide comes in and sweeps them off the ice flow and into the water and all the penguin babies learn to swim.

Fortunately for us, the Universe will not let us say no to our soul purpose too long. We can eagerly jump off the edge of our current reality, fret and fume before we leap, or we can refuse to move at all, but eventually the Great Creator will win out. The choice is ours. Life is not static. It moves us forward towards whatever we are focused on—hopefully, our soul purpose.

There is no more beautiful description of this process than what Dr. Ernest Holmes, great turn-of-the-century philosopher, once wrote:

> *Nature will not let us stay in one place too long.*
> *She will let us stay just long enough to gather the*
> *experience necessary to the unfolding and ad-*
> *vancement of the soul. This is a wise provision, for*
> *should we stay here too long, we would become too*
> *set, too rigid, too inflexible. Nature demands the*
> *change in order that we may advance. When the*
> *change comes, we should welcome it with a smile*
> *on the lips and a song in the heart.*

Rediscovering your soul purpose is a journey with no beginning and no end. Remember, with every step you take and every breath you make, you have within you all the answers. Along the way, don't forget to stop often and celebrate who you are!

The Rest Of The Story . . .

As I stood at my father's grave along with other family members, I remembered the last conversation I had with him. His journey of recovery had taken him to a nursing home where he lived out the remainder of his life.

One night, late in the evening, the phone rang. It was the nursing home staff informing me that my father had fallen that day and hurt himself quite badly. After making the necessary decisions for his well-being, the nurse handed the phone to Dad. My father asked how I was and what I was doing with my life. As I shared with him the successes I was experiencing, he very quietly said, "I'm real proud of you, Sweetheart. You have done something with your life . . . something I never could do." I heard his voice crack. "What is that Dad," I asked.

"I could never believe in myself . . ." he whispered with emotion in his voiced. I waited. "I let other people tell me I was no good and let alcohol steal my dreams, rob me of my talents and destroy my life. I'd better go now . . . but just remember, I love you."

I hung up the phone slowly, giving thanks for such a precious moment. I decided right then that I would continue to love myself enough to make my soul purpose the primary focus for the rest of my life.

❖   ❖   ❖

Glossary

Analyzer	that part of you that probes, prods and logically analyzes all aspects of your life.
Being of Service	to give away and share your divinely-given talents with the rest of humanity.
Being Powerless	a state of being a victim; hiding who you truly are so that others will approve of you.
Career	work for which you have been trained but which may or may not fulfill you.
Creative Child	the untamed, passionate, wild and gutsy part of yourself—often stifled.
Creativity	the expression of your divine energies.
Critical Voice	the voice inside you that regularly comments (usually negatively) on what it thinks of you and your behavior.
Divine Discontent	a feeling of restlessness, edginess and irritability without any apparent cause—brought on by your genius self nudging you into making changes in your life.
Foundational Support System	it is made up of people you admire, ideas which inspire and motivate you, and personal friends who can give you support when things get tough.
Genius Creativity	the conscious awareness and expression of your creative powers and divine energies.
Genius Self	the state of living your soul purpose.

Genius Treasure Map	a poster board containing pictures, drawings and sayings that are a physical representation of your desired manifestations.
Great Creator	the divine power and creative source of the universe; known by many names: God, the Great Spirit, Yahweh, Allah and others.
Higher Self	your soul or True Self—the spiritual essence embodied in all humans.
Job	an activity you do to earn money.
Law of Subconscious Activity	as soon as the subconscious mind accepts an idea, it immediately begins to create a pattern that will result in the realization of this idea.
Letter of Legacy	a eulogy written by you for your funeral, set in the undefined future, describing your best qualities and (ideal) accomplishments. It allows you to create the life you want to have lived by the time you transition.
Living a Life of Success	when you are expressing your creative energies and doing what you love to do, you are living a life of success.
Manifesting	creating something in this physical reality through the use of our thoughts, imagination and focus. Things can be manifested intentionally, when one is aware of our ability to do so, and unintentionally, when one is not aware.
Negative Personal Power	is self-centered and egotistical; controls and coerces others to get what he or she wants.
Observer Self	that part of you that only notices, but does not judge

or analyze, what goes on in your life.

Positive Personal Power	being in charge of your own life; expressing who you really are in spite of others' opinions; taking care of your own needs without negatively impacting others.
Sacred Circle	an exercise designed to increase self-awareness.
Skills	things you have learned to do, but which may or may not be things you like to do.
Soul	the spiritual essence embodied in all human beings, a person's total self. This is sometimes called one's true self or higher self.
Soul Purpose	an intention to express your spiritual essence . . . to express your total self in your life. When you are expressing your soul purpose, you have stepped into your genius self.
Soul Purpose Work	the expression of one's spiritual essence and one's destiny; it is fulfilling, fun and financially rewarding.
Soul Qualities	aspects of life that you value, and that you want or already have in your life.
Talents	things you are innately good at doing and which make you happy when you are doing them.
Transitioning	leaving one's body at the moment of physical death and moving into the next realm.
True Self	your soul or higher self—the spiritual essence embodied in all humans.